PREDICTIVE TECHNIQUES AND THE APPLICATION OF ASTROLOGICAL REMEDIAL MEASURES
(Based on Systems' Approach)

By:

V.K. Choudhry, MBA.
K. Rajesh Chaudhary, MBA.

Salient Features:

*Predictive Techniques *Astral Remedies *Impact of Evil Lords and Planets in Evil Houses *Timing of Events *Recovery of Patients *Return of Missing Persons *Financial Prosperity *Handling Psychiatric Problems, Delay in Marriage, Stability in Marriage *Identifying Early Widowhood and Criminal Tendencies *Relocation through Astrology *Relevance of Vastu to Astrology

PREDICTIVE TECHNIQUES AND THE APPLICATION OF ASTROLOGICAL REMEDIAL MEASURES
(Based on Systems' Approach)

Salient Features:
*Predictive Techniques *Astral Remedies *Impact of Evil Lords and Planets in Evil Houses *Timing of Events *Recovery of Patients *Return of Missing Persons *Financial Prosperity *Handling Psychiatric Problems, Delay in Marriage, Stability in Marriage *Identifying Early Widowhood and Criminal Tendencies *Relocation through Astrology *Relevance of Vastu to Astrology

Author:
V. K. Choudhry
M.B.A., Founder Chairman,
International Institute of Predictive Astrology,
Fairfield, USA, and Propounder of Systems' Approach for
Interpreting Horoscopes

Co-Author:
K. Rajesh Chaudhary
M.B.A., Vice President,
India Chapter, International Institute of Predictive Astrology,
Fairfield, USA

Sagar Publications
72, Janpath, Ved Mansion, New Delhi-110001
Tel.: 23320648, 23328245
E-mail: sagarpub@vsnl.com
Website: www.sagarpublications.com

1st Published 1997 Reprinted 2001
Revised Edition 2006

Revised and Updated Edition 2014

Published and Printed by:
Saurabh Sagar for **Sagar Publications** New Delhi-110001

and

Printed at:
The Artwaves, New Delhi-110019, Telfax.: 41609709;
E-mail: theartwaves@gmail.com

ABOUT THE AUTHORS

Shri V. K. Choudhry

(Propounder of the Systems' Approach for Interpreting Horoscopes)

V. K. Choudhry

Shri V.K. Choudhry, well known in the field of Vedic Astrology through his many books and articles, was conferred the title of Jyotish Martund by the International Council of Astrological and Occult Studies, Hyderabad (India) in 1989; the title of Jyotish Kovid by the Indian Council of Astrological Sciences, Madras, in 1991; and the title of Jyotish Bhanu by Astro Sciences Research Organization, New Delhi, in 1992. He has been a faculty member and Chapter Course Director (Astrology) with ICAS.

Shri Choudhry is the recipient of Pracharya Award (Professor of Astrology) conferred by Bharat Nirman in December, 1993, for his outstanding and excellent contributions in the field of Astrology. In 1994, his name was listed in "Indo American Who's Who", in recognition of his contributions for predictive accuracy in Vedic Astrology.

Shri Choudhry participated in the 10th International Seminar of Astrology and Occult Science from 11th to 13th of June 1995, at Hyderabad and delivered lectures on "Timing of Events" and "Vastu Shastra". Shri Choudhry was conferred the title of "Master of Astrology" in this Seminar by International Council of Astrological and Occult Studies.

The Board of Directors of International Council of Alternative Medicines conferred the degree of Doctor of Alternative Medical Sciences on Shri Choudhry on 3rd of February 1996, at Bombay. The International Institute of Astrology & Occultism, New Delhi, conferred a Gold Medal and the honorary title of Jyotish Vachaspathi on Shri Choudhry in April 1996, at New Delhi.

International Foundation of Peace, Fraternity and Humanistic, Bombay, conferred the title of Dharam Yogi in 1995. International Council of Astrological Sciences, Bombay, conferred the title of Vastu Shastra Samrat in 1996, and Bhartiya Ved Jyotish Vigyan Sansthan, Modinagar (India), conferred the title of Sthapatya Ratna in 1996, on Shri Choudhry for his valuable contributions in the fields of Astrology and Vastu Shastra. Prof Choudhry participated in astrological conferences in London, Paris and U.S.A.

His managerial background has enabled him to use modern communicative skills in so systematic a manner that the comprehension of predictive techniques has been greatly simplified. His book, "Self Learning Course in Astrology" makes learning of the "Systems' Approach" methodology a simple step-by-step process and has proved to be of great help to both the serious students as well as the practitioners still plagued by the confusing inconsistencies in the classical texts.

United Cultural Convention, North Caroline, USA, sealed the nomination of Prof. V. K. Choudhry for receipt of the 2002 Noble Prize for Outstanding Achievement and Contributions to Humanity. This nomination stems from extensive research on extraordinary leaders by the top officials of the United Cultural Convention.

American Biographical Institute inducted Mr. Vinod Kumar Choudhry to the Hall of Fame in July, 2009, for Distinguished Accomplishments in Astrology and for dedication and efforts that have left an indelible mark on the lives of others.

Vedic Astrologer & Author Shri K. Rajesh Chaudhary

Mr. K Rajesh Chaudhary, MBA, Astrologer & Author is Vice President of Indian Chapter, International Institute of Predictive Astrology, Fairfield, USA.

Delhi Astro Study Circle (Registered) New Delhi, conferred the honorary title of Jyotish Martund on Shri Chaudhary in 2011.

He participated in free astrological clinics held in New Delhi by Bharat Nirman in 1994 - 1995. He has been key person for organizing presentations made in the International Conferences of SA Astrologers in Gurgaon. He is Director of the Systems' Institute of Hindu Astrology (SIHA).

K. Rajesh Chaudhary

Indian Institute of Oriental Heritage, Kolkata, India, conferred Life Time Achievement Award on Shri Chaudhary on 7th March, 2014.

The analysis in this book are based on the Systems' Approach for Interpreting Horoscopes.

He is co-author for the following successful books:

1. Self Learning Course in Astrology.

2. Systems' Approach for Interpreting Horoscopes

3. Select Right Profession through Astrology.

4. How to Study Divisional Charts

5. A complete book on Medical Astrology.

6. How to Analyze Married Life.

7. Impact of Ascending Zodiac Signs.

8.   Triple Transit Influence of Planets.

9.   A complete book on Horary Astrology.

10. Predictive Techniques in Astrology.

Website: www.YourNetAstrologer.com
Website: www.JyotishRemedies121.com

SAGAR PUBLICATIONS

PREFACE

With mounting stresses and strains in the modern society, more and more people are turning towards astrology for precise predictions and astrological remedial measures to reduce risks and tensions and to harness the positive traits. Though the malefic impact cannot be removed completely, regular performance of astrology remedies help in reducing the impact significantly.

New trends in the astrological applications are emerging in the fields of human resource development, scanning of macro environment for investments, setting up of new offices and joint ventures, timing of operations, developing leadership skills, developing concentration for studies, seeking help for emotional stability, seeking help for chronic diseases and prime sterility, analysis of aptitudes of children, etc.

Success in any field depends upon the leadership qualities. The various traits of a dynamic personality are governed by various planets. For example, for organizing, acquiring and cultivating a diligent team one requires a strong Sun in one's horoscope. The strong mooltrikona sign lords of the second and third houses also act as the Sun. Jupiter rules dependability, honesty and knowledge while Mars rules enterprising and aggressive persuasions. The public relations and imagination is ruled by the Moon while interactivity, team work and tolerance is ruled by Venus. The integrity is ruled by the Sun and Jupiter while the analytical and communicative capabilities are ruled by the planet, Mercury. If any of the planets is weak in the horoscope, the traits ruled by the said planet remain weak endangering or delaying success and result in partial success. To avoid picking up of the negative traits of net picking, viciousness, rudeness and increased excitability and harnessing of the positive traits, astrology offers strengthening of concerned weak planets.

Keeping in view the rising demands of the society, predictive techniques and the application of astrological remedial measures have been elaborated in this book for the practicing astrologers and the advance learners. We hope the readers will find the book to their satisfaction.

The Systems' Approach incorporates some changes in the fundamentals of classical Astrology. The fundamental changes have been suggested with definite reasons. The aim is to achieve predictive accuracy and for this, the Systems' Approach is dependable. The fundamental changes have been suggested to simplify analysis. This approach is universally applicable to all horoscopes with one single technique of analysis. This enables one to identify the area of a problem, the positive traits, the strengths and weaknesses of various planetary configurations right at birth without any explanation given by the person seeking astrological consultation.

The Systems' Approach explains why the second house is connected with education. It also explains as to why for those born in Cancer ascendant, the significations of the various houses as well as the planets are adversely affected when they are closely conjunct or aspected by Jupiter and Saturn.

Birth particulars have been withheld in some case studies out of respect for the privacy of the natives, even though the inclusion of such charts has been considered necessary.

V.K. Choudhry
K. Rajesh Chaudhary

105, A-Block, South City- II
Gurgaon-122018 (India)
Ph. : 91-9811016333, 91-9899417444
E-mail: vkchoudhry@gmail.com
Website: http//www.YourNetAstrologer.com

CONTENTS

S. No.	**Description**	Page No.

Chapter 1

Advanced Predictive Techniques and Salient Features of Systems' Approach

The divine science of astrology is a wonderful asset to the mankind. It unfolds the future, reduces tensions and enables one to move in the right direction. It helps us for taking decisions in the face of uncertainties. It deals with various aspects of human life such as health - physical and mental, business, social status, financial prosperity, name and fame, relationships, progeny, employment, emotional stability, etc. The predictive astrology gives us firm indications in life pertaining to the future events, right at birth. The preventive astrological remedial measures at the same time help us by reducing the impact of unfavorable planetary influences and harnessing the significations ruled by functional benefic planets.

Astrology, the ancient wisdom, helps us in understanding the potentialities and weaknesses of our personality to enable us to charter the course of success in our life in the matters of health, career, love, relationships and finances. The horoscope influences are studied through the natal conjunctions, aspects and placements of planets read in conjunction with the planetary strengths, planetary periods - dasa (main period), bhukti (sub-period) and current planetary influences (transit) with reference to the ascending sign. The ascending sign is worked out on the basis of the birth date, time and place. The conjunctions and aspects help us in identifying the auspicious and inauspicious planetary configurations. The placement of a planet links the significations of the house ruled by it with the significations of the house where it is placed. An afflicted planet indicates suffering through the significations ruled by the said planet. The blessed ones are impelled by the divine forces for making use of the ultimate knowledge and Astrological Remedial Measures (Jyotish Remedies) - both propitiating functional malefic planets and strengthening weak functional benefic planets through "Kavach" or "Special Power Kavach" or gemstones. Based on the planetary influences in a birth chart/ horoscope, preventive Jyotish Remedies both propitiatory and use of Kavach or Special Power Kavach, as necessary, are suggested.

The world dreads AIDS, cancer, cardio-vascular diseases, psychiatric problems, auto-immune disorders, etc. The modern systems of medicine whether allopathic and/or alternative medicines offer us guiding factors for preventing these dreaded diseases or early detection of these so that these can respond to symptomatic treatment. No science/system other than astrology has the twin capacity (i) to forewarn about vulnerability of the person to severe problems; and (ii) forearm to avoid the impact of strong afflictions resulting into problems. The divine science of astrology offers the preventive peace making remedies for such diseases wherever possibility of such a disease is indicated.

We come across malfunctioning of functional health at the time of birth where the individual concerned has no role to play in abuse of his/her food habits, etc. Astrology relates it to the deeds of the past life based on the theory of Karma. We are not trying to create here any orthodoxy or blind faith or fatalism. We wish to share with you our experience in the application of the science of astrology in the administration of preventive and curative astrological remedies, timing of the diseases and recovery.

The timing is done with the help of the horoscope. The horoscope is a record of the planetary positions prevailing at the time of the birth of a particular person at a particular place. This knowledge is the most valuable gift of ancient wisdom to mankind. All sciences depend on the experience by way of observations and analysis of logical hypothesis developed and tested based on these observations. It is really painful when such a useful gift to mankind is just termed as a superstition without even giving astrology a trial by the so-called rationalists.

Despite phenomenal growth in the modern healing sciences, permanent cure for the functional health problems, be it in the fields of psychological problems, cardiovascular problems, renal problems, asthmatic problems, liver problems, immunization power of the body, sleep disorders, etc., has not been found. Astrology offers us preventive diagnostic power and astral remedies both for preventive and curative measures. Administering medicine is supported manifold when combined with the astral remedies. The operating planetary periods indicate the time frame for recovery. This in turn gives patience and results of the symptomatic treatment both to the doctor and the patient.

Salient Features of the Systems' Approach

For the benefit of the readers, the prominent features of the Systems' Approach are being discussed here. Events/indications in life are ruled by the interplay of the planets, houses, signs and planetary periods. The planets during their operating periods bless the person with the significations ruled by them depending upon their strength and placement in a particular horoscope. Identifying the weakness/affliction of planets is not at all a difficult job and can be learnt by beginners or non-astrologers with the help of the techniques given in this book. The Systems' Approach not only increases the accuracy of analysis but also speeds up the analytical process. It helps in identifying the results of analysis in an unambiguous manner, consistently and without any confusion.

If the medical personnel learn Vedic Astrology, their dual competence will help humanity at large and will enhance satisfaction and personal eminence of the medical practitioners. Besides the protection from dreaded diseases through preventive astral remedies, the astral remedies tackle the problems of sterility, impotency, help in getting a healthy male child in addition to other areas of life governed by the same planet e.g. professional growth, harmonious married life, acquisition of wealth/property and status. For example, one with defects in the right eye suffers in his professional growth, suffers from loss of status, problems in married life and would be vulnerable to cardiovascular diseases, thyroid glands, etc. At the same time, one with phenomenal ambitions would be vulnerable to nervous breakdown, acidity and runs the risk of a paralytic attack. We hope this gives a clear understanding of the linkage between the planetary strengths and diseases, general problems in life, etc.

The key issues in horoscope analysis are:

1)   Identifying the functional nature of planets in a birth chart;

2)   The techniques for judging the strength of a planet;

3)   The distinction between weak planets and afflicted planets;

4)   The impact of weak and/or afflicted planets;

5)   The orb of longitudinal difference for judging the impact of conjunctions and aspects;

6)   The most malefic influence;

7)   The most effective point of various houses in a horoscope.

Functional Nature of Planets

The functional nature of planets is the key analytical factor in the horoscope analysis. Besides Rahu and Ketu, the planets, whose mooltrikona signs are in malefic houses (sixth, eighth and twelfth) with reference to the ascendant, act as functional malefic planets in a birth chart. For this purpose, under the Systems' Approach the sign Cancer is considered as the mooltrikona sign of the Moon.

For various ascending signs, the functional malefic planets are mentioned hereunder:

Ascendant	Functional Malefic Planets
1. Aries	Mercury, Rahu and Ketu.
2. Taurus	Venus, Jupiter, Mars, Rahu and Ketu.
3. Gemini	Rahu and Ketu.
4. Cancer	Jupiter, Saturn, Rahu and Ketu.
5. Leo	The Moon, Rahu and Ketu.
6. Virgo	Saturn, Mars, the Sun, Rahu and Ketu.
7. Libra	Mercury, Rahu and Ketu.
8. Scorpio	Mars, Venus, Rahu and Ketu.
9. Sagittarius	The Moon, Rahu and Ketu.
10. Capricorn	The Sun, Jupiter, Rahu and Ketu.
11. Aquarius	The Moon, Mercury, Rahu and Ketu.
12. Pisces	The Sun, Venus, Saturn, Rahu and Ketu.

The functional nature of any planet depends on the nature of the mooltrikona house of that planet. It is not related to the strength of the planet. A planet may be weak or strong but the functional nature will remain same as per the defined principle for identifying the functional nature of planets.

North Indian Chart Style

This is the best form of drawing a chart as it provides a very easy comprehension of the chart at a mere glimpse. It shows angles/planets placed in angles without enumeration.

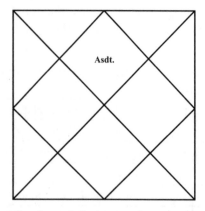

Even identification of the houses is very easy in this form of a birth chart. The houses are always fixed and are shown below:

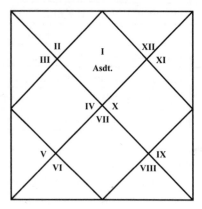

Angular houses have been marked hereunder:

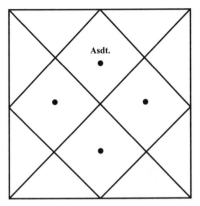

It shows whether any planet is posited in the malefic houses. The sixth, eighth and twelfth houses in a chart are known as malefic houses. Malefic houses have been marked hereunder:

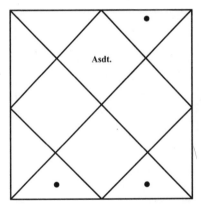

It shows the placement of planets in trines, if any, at a mere glimpse. The trinal positions have been shown as under:

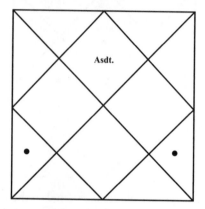

Even reckoning of the aspects is very easy in this form of a birth chart. The houses are always fixed and are shown below:

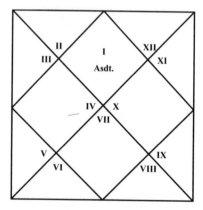

According with Systems' Approach, the lordship of the houses is reckoned from the placement of a mooltrikona sign in a particular house. The lord of the mooltrikona sign placed in a particular house is called the lord of the house. The counting of houses is done in an anti clockwise direction. In the following chart, for example, the sign Gemini rises in the ascendant:

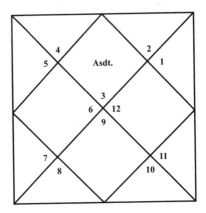

As the sign Libra is placed in the fifth house, Venus will be the lord of the fifth house.

South Indian Chart Style

In the South Indian Chart, the signs are fixed while the ascendant has to be written in the sign where the ascending sign rises. For example, if the Gemini rises in the ascendant the South Indian Chart will be as under.

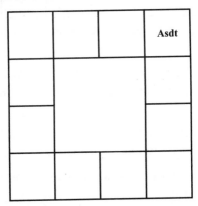

The house indicating the ascendant is the first house and the other houses are counted in the clockwise direction.

Conjunction

Conjunction is the apparent coincidence or proximity of two or more celestial objects as viewed from the earth. The conjunction can be exact or close. If the difference in longitudes happens to be less than one degree, the resulting conjunction is known as an exact conjunction. If the difference in longitudes is within five degrees, the same is known as a close conjunction.

Example Chart 1

This example is given for clear understanding of the exact or close conjunctions.

In this chart the planets Venus and Mars are in exact conjunction in the ascendant as their longitude difference is less than one degree.

The planets Sun and Jupiter are in close conjunction as their longitude difference is within five degrees.

The Moon is in exact conjunction to the most effective point of the second house.

Though Jupiter and Mercury are in the first and second houses, respectively, but they are in exact conjunction as their longitude difference is within one degree.

Aspects

The aspects are partial and full. In the Vedic system of Astrology, we are concerned with only full aspects. Each planet is believed to aspect fully the seventh house, reckoned / counted from the placement of the former.

In addition to the seventh aspect, planets posited outside the orbit of the earth (Mars, Jupiter and Saturn) as well as Rahu and Ketu have additional special full aspects as under:

• Saturn aspects third and tenth houses from its location.

• Mars aspects fourth and eighth houses from its location.

• Jupiter, Rahu and Ketu aspect fifth and ninth houses from their location.

Planets influence other houses/planets aspected by them favorably or unfavorably, depending upon their functional nature in the horoscope. The principle of exact or close aspect is identical to exact or close conjunction i.e. when a planet casts its aspect on another planet(s) or on the most effective point of house(s) within an orb of one degree, the aspect is known as an exact aspect. If the difference in planetary longitudes is within five degrees, then the aspect is known as a close aspect.

Example Chart 2

Ke21°59'		Ma3°20'	**11°25' Asdt**
Ve9°20'			Mo22°6'
Me11° Su19°31'			
Sa9°44'	Ju5°46'		Ra21°59'

This example is given for clear understanding of the exact or close aspects.

In this chart the planet Rahu closely aspects the Sun with fifth aspect as the longitude difference is less than five degrees.

The planets Mars and Jupiter mutually form close aspect as their aspect longitude difference is within five degrees.

Mercury forms exact aspect to the most effective point of the second house. This is the seventh aspect of Mercury.

Ketu forms exact aspect to the Moon placed in the second house. This is fifth aspect of Ketu to the Moon from the tenth house.

Saturn forms exact aspect to Venus as the longitude difference is less than one degree between the longitude of the two planets. This is third aspect of Saturn from seventh house to Venus placed in the ninth house.

Saturn forms close aspect to the most effective point of the ascendant as the longitude difference is less than five degrees between the longitude of Saturn and the ascendant. This is seventh aspect of Saturn from the seventh house to the ascendant.

Wide Conjunction or Aspects

The conjunctions or aspects with more than five degrees of longitudinal difference are wide conjunctions or aspects. These do not have permanent impact in life except the short lived transit influences on the planets involved in wide conjunctions or aspects. The wide aspects give their results in later part of life, say around 60 years or after.

The aspect of a functional benefic planet will be effective corresponding to the strength of the planet(s)/house(s) involved. If the aspecting functional benefic planet is weak due to any reason including debilitation its effectiveness will be weak and limited, but its close aspect will always act as a helping force. The close aspect of a functional malefic planet, except on the most effective point of its mooltrikona house, will always act as a damaging force.

General and Particular Significations of Planets

The general significations of a planet mean the aspects ruled by that planet. For example, the Sun rules father, status of the person, job, heart, digestive system, etc., irrespective of the lordship of the Sun in a particular birth chart.

The particular significations of a planet mean the significations of its mooltrikona sign house in the natal chart. If the sign Leo rises in the third house then the Sun will rule the third house. The significations of the third house will be known as particular significations of the Sun.

The results of the significations of a weak planet fructify with delay and suffer whenever that weak planet is afflicted due to close aspect or conjunction with any functional malefic planet. The natal affliction causes damages in the entire sub-periods of the weak planet and the afflicting planets. The transit affliction causes short term damages during the effective transit influence.

Dispositor

According to the Systems' Approach, the dispositor is a planet in whose mooltrikona sign another planet is located in the natal chart. Suppose in a natal chart the Sun is placed in the sign Libra ruled by Venus. In this case Venus will be the dispositor of the Sun. No planet which is in a non-mooltrikona sign will have a dispositor i.e. the planet(s) in Taurus, Gemini, Scorpio, Capricorn and Pisces have no dispositor. If a planet is posited in Aries, its dispositor would be Mars; if a planet is posited in Cancer, its dispositor would be the Moon; if a planet is posited in Leo, its dispositor would be the Sun; if a planet is posited in Virgo, its dispositor would be Mercury; if a planet is posited in Libra, its dispositor would be Venus; if a planet is posited in Sagittarius, its dispositor would be Jupiter; and if a planet is posited in Aquarius, its dispositor would be Saturn.

When a functional benefic planet becomes dispositor of an affliction, the results of such affliction will surface during the sub period and transit influence of that functional benefic planet. Similarly, when a functional benefic planet becomes dispositor of a benefic influence or blessing, the results of such benefic influence or blessing will surface during the sub period and transit influence of that functional benefic planet.

When a functional malefic planet becomes dispositor of a benefic influence or blessing, the results of such benefic influence or blessing will also simultaneously surface during the sub period and transit influence of that functional malefic planet provided the functional malefic planet is not involved in a close or exact affliction.

When a functional malefic planet becomes dispositor of an affliction, the results of such affliction will also surface during the sub period and transit influence of that functional malefic planet.

When a functional malefic planet becomes dispositor of an affliction, the results of such affliction will also be suffered by those planets for whom it becomes dispositor. Suppose Venus is afflicted in a birth chart and the planets Jupiter and the Moon are placed in the sign Libra. In this case the impact of affliction will also be passed on to the Moon and Jupiter.

While finding out the strength of a planet we always find out the strength of its ultimate dispositor.

Special Impact of Rahu and Ketu

In exceptional cases, when Rahu is well placed in a mooltrikona sign of a planet, without causing any conjunction or close aspect with other houses and planets and its dispositor is strong, Rahu gives good results during its sub-periods for materialistic prosperity. Rahu-Ketu, when exalted, give materialist benefits while debilitated Rahu involves the person in exposed scandals and acute physical sufferings.

The functional malefic planets for various ascendants, mentioned above, may appear to be at variance when seen in the context of the available classical texts, but when you analyze the charts based on the functional malefic planets brought out hereinabove, you would find that all of your confusions disappear at one stroke. The classical principles were laid down by Maharishi Parashara in Dwapara yuga and changes, mutatis mutandis (wherever necessary) have been suggested for the nativities in Kaliyuga.

The functional benefic planets for various ascending signs are as under:

Ascendant	Functional Benefic Planets
1. Aries	The Sun, the Moon, Mars, Jupiter, Venus and Saturn.
2. Taurus	The Sun, the Moon, Mercury and Saturn.
3. Gemini	The Sun, the Moon, Mars, Mercury, Jupiter, Venus and Saturn.
4. Cancer	The Sun, the Moon, Mars, Mercury, and Venus.
5. Leo	The Sun, Mars, Mercury, Jupiter, Venus and Saturn.
6. Virgo	The Moon, Mercury, Jupiter and Venus.
7. Libra	The Sun, the Moon, Mars, Jupiter, Venus and Saturn.
8. Scorpio	The Sun, the Moon, Mercury, Jupiter and Saturn.
9. Sagittarius	The Sun, Mars, Mercury, Jupiter, Venus and Saturn.
10. Capricorn	The Moon, Mars, Mercury, Venus and Saturn.
11. Aquarius	The Sun, Mars, Jupiter, Venus and Saturn.
12. Pisces	The Moon, Mars, Mercury and Jupiter.

Afflicted Planets or Houses

The afflictions to the planets or houses are caused by the close conjunction or aspect of the functional malefic planets in a birth chart. Whenever a planet or a mooltrikona house is already weak for any other reason and is under the close influence of any functional malefic, it is treated as an afflicted planet/house. But when the planet or the mooltrikona house is not weak for other reasons, it can be considered afflicted either under the exact influence of a functional malefic for normal afflictions or under the orb of influence of two degrees for special/multiple afflictions, becoming a weak planet/house for that reason. **So whenever any planet or mooltrikona house is afflicted, it becomes weak not being capable of fully protecting/promoting its significations. The significations of the houses having mooltrikona sign of an afflicted planet are harmed more when such planets are already weak for other reasons.**

Whenever a non-mooltrikona house is under the close influence of any functional malefic, it is treated as an afflicted house.

If not placed in its own mooltrikona sign, any planet becomes afflicted just by mere placement in any of the dusthanas/malefic houses.

Afflicting Planets

It is very necessary to understand the difference between afflicting planets and afflicted planets.

All planets can become afflicted, but only the functional malefic planets can be afflicting planets.

A transit functional malefic planet will always afflict its natal position by conjunction or aspect, except when placed in its own mooltrikona house in rasi/birth chart. A natal/transit functional malefic planet never afflicts its own mooltrikona house, except when the functional malefic planet is already afflicted and afflicts from a dusthana/malefic house. Dispositor weakness or bad placement affliction is not applicable in this case. The benefit of aspect to the mooltrikona sign of a functional malefic planet is limited to the proportion of the strength of the functional malefic planet.

The Most Effective Point of a House

Besides the natal position of the planets, there is the most effective point (MEP) of each house known by the degree rising in the ascendant. The close impact of the planets in the case of houses is gauged through their closeness to the natal positions. Suppose an ascendant of 16 degrees rises. It means the most effective point of each house would be 16 degrees. In case the lord of a mooltrikona house is weak or in case of non-mooltrikona houses, a functional malefic planet having a longitude between 11 to 21 degrees will afflict these houses either by placement or by aspect. In case the lord of a mooltrikona house is "otherwise" strong, that house will only become afflicted under the single influence of a functional malefic planet having a longitude between 15 to 17 degrees, or under the multiple/special influence of functional malefic planet(s) having longitudes between 14 to 18 degrees. That "otherwise" strong lord will become weak for this reason. The influence of any functional malefic planet over its own mooltrikona house will never be malefic, by way of close conjunction to the MEP.

Let us see this concept for clarity through an example chart given below. Some of the aspects discussed in this example like conjunctions, aspects, weak planets, strong planets, are explained.

Example Chart 3

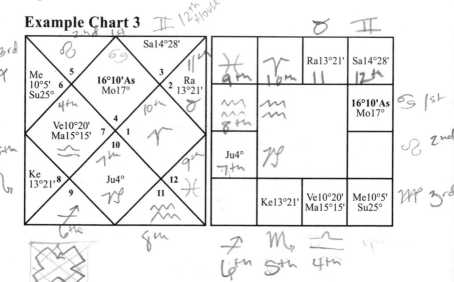

In the above chart the rising degree of the ascendant is 16°10'. This 16°10' becomes the most effective point (MEP) of each house. Now we will see the application of close aspects, close conjunctions, exact conjunctions, exact aspects, single afflictions, special afflictions and multiple afflictions in the above chart.

The Sun is placed in the third house. Therefore, the orb of affliction for the second house by a single functional malefic planet is one degree. There is no functional malefic planet which afflicts the second house within an orb of one degree. Now, the second house can be afflicted by a special affliction or multiple afflictions within an orb of two degrees. We find that the second house MEP is under the special affliction of the most malefic planet, Saturn, from the twelfth house within an orb of two degrees. This affliction not only afflicts the second house, but also make the otherwise strong Sun, weak, due to afflictions to its mooltrikona sign house. Once becoming weak, the second house becomes vulnerable to natal or transit afflictions within an orb of five degrees on either side of the MEP.

The Moon is strongly placed in the ascendant and it forms an exact conjunction with the MEP of the ascendant. It forms an exact aspect to the MEP of the seventh house. The Moon and MEP of the ascendant becomes vulnerable to transit afflictions within an orb of one degree

Mercury is strongly placed in its mooltrikona sign in the third house. There is no natal affliction to the third house and natal Mercury. Natal Mercury and MEP of the third house becomes vulnerable to transit afflictions within an orb of one degree

Jupiter is weak in the chart as (i) it is in its sign of debilitation (ii) its mooltrikona sign is under special affliction of the most malefic planet, Saturn, from the twelfth house; and (iii) it is in the state of infancy. Therefore, both Jupiter and the sixth house are vulnerable to natal and transit afflictions within an orb of five degrees.

$15° \underline{\frown}$

The functional benefic planet Mars is strongly placed in the fourth house and it closely and beneficially influences the houses occupied and aspected. Therefore, both Mars and the tenth house ʏ are vulnerable to natal or transit afflictions within an orb of one degree.

$10° \underline{\frown}$

The functional benefic planet Venus is strongly placed in the fourth house and it beneficially influences the fourth house. Therefore, both Venus and the fourth house are vulnerable to natal or transit afflictions within an orb of one degree.

The most malefic planet Saturn is weak as it is badly placed. It severely afflicts the houses occupied and aspected. Both Saturn and the eighth house are vulnerable to natal or transit affliction within an orb of five degrees on either side.

Rahu and Ketu form close afflictions to the eleventh, fifth, seventh and Ninth houses as the orb of afflictions for the non-mooltrikona sign houses is five degrees on either side of the MEP.

Hope this example helps you in understanding the concepts of the most effective point of the house(s), special afflictions and multiple afflictions through close or exact conjunctions / aspects. This will go a long way in your understanding the case studies included in this book and our other books.

The Most Malefic Influence

Mostly, the people seeking advantage of Astrology remember it in the time of distress. Therefore, the first thing is to gauge the strength of the planets so that the influences of functional malefic planets on the weak planets can be analyzed. The most malefic influence in a birth chart is that of the most malefic planet.

Most Malefic Planet

If there is a mooltrikona sign in the eighth house from the ascendant, its lord is called the most malefic planet (MMP). In case there is no mooltrikona sign in the eighth house then the role of the most malefic planet is played by the lord of the twelfth house containing a mooltrikona sign. If there is no mooltrikona sign in the twelfth house, too, then the role of the most malefic planet is played by Ketu. For various ascendants the most malefic planets are as under:

Ascendant	Most Malefic Planet
Aries	Ketu
Taurus	Jupiter
Gemini	Ketu
Cancer	Saturn
Leo	The Moon
Virgo	Mars
Libra	Mercury
Scorpio	Venus
Sagittarius	The Moon
Capricorn	The Sun
Aquarius	Mercury
Pisces	Venus

If the planet or the lord of the house, with which the most malefic planet is forming a close conjunction/aspect, is strong, this most malefic planet creates tension(s) with regard to the matters represented by the house/planet involved. When the afflicted planet is weak, the significations suffer seriously. When the afflicted planet is badly placed, it results in tragic happenings. To understand the difference between tension, serious trouble and tragic happenings consider the situations of fever, jaundice and the loss of a limb ruled by the concerned planet, respectively. Any affliction caused by the triple transit triggering influence of a functional malefic planet can trigger the trouble, especially if it involves a slow moving planet in transit. When the affliction is close to the most effective point of the house, significations of all the houses involved, that is the house occupied and the house(s) aspected, suffer. In the case of the afflicted planets, besides their general significations, the significations of the house where the mooltrikona sign is placed, and the significations of the house where the planet is placed, also suffer.

The Most Benefic Influence

If there is a mooltrikona sign in the fourth house from the ascendant, its lord is called the most benefic planet (MBP). In case there is no mooltrikona sign in the fourth house, then the role of the most benefic planet is played by the lord of the second house containing the mooltrikona sign. In case there is no mooltrikona sign in the second house as well, then the role of the most benefic planet is played by the lord of the ninth house containing the ♀ ☿ mooltrikona sign. If there is no mooltrikona sign in the ninth house, too, then the role of the most benefic planet is played by the lord of the third house containing the mooltrikona sign. For various ascendants the most benefic planets are as under:

Ascendant	Most Benefic Planet
Aries	The Moon
Taurus	The Sun
Gemini	Mercury
Cancer	Venus
Leo	Mercury
Virgo	Jupiter
Libra	Jupiter
Scorpio	Saturn
Sagittarius	The Sun
Capricorn	Mars
Aquarius	Venus
Pisces	Mars

Effective Orb for Judging the Influence of Natal/Transit Conjunctions/Aspects

In the case of influence of functional malefic planets over the most effective points of mooltrikona houses/planets simultaneously strong in rasi and transit, the orb is one degree on either side for normal afflictions and two degrees on either side for special/multiple afflictions, while in the case of mooltrikona houses/planets either weak in rasi or in transit, the orb is five degrees on either side.

In the case of influence of strong functional benefic planets over the most effective points of mooltrikona houses/planets simultaneously strong in rasi and transit, the orb is five degrees on either side, while in the case of mooltrikona houses/planets either weak in rasi or in transit, the orb is one degree on either side. Under the influence of natal/transit functional malefic planets, all planets get malefically influenced.

The maximum influence of the transit or natal conjunction/ aspect is when it is within one degree on either side. As soon as the transit influence starts separating, the influence starts tapering down. It is very important to see the strength of the planet on which the transit influence is being studied. For example, if the Sun, being the lord of the fourth house, is placed in the fourth house and its longitude is eleven degrees and is strong, the functional malefic influence of Jupiter, the most malefic planet for the Taurus ascendant, will be effective when Jupiter is between 9 degrees and 13 degrees in the signs Leo, Sagittarius, Aquarius or Aries, while the single functional malefic influence of Mars will be effective when Mars is between 10 degrees and 12 degrees in the signs Leo, Capricorn, Aquarius or Taurus, because the Sun is strong in the natal chart. Please do not forget to consider the transit strength of this Sun. If the Sun in a Taurus birth chart is placed in the sign Libra at a longitude of five degrees then the transit influence of Jupiter over it would be effective whenever Jupiter transits from zero degrees to 10 degrees in Libra, Aquarius, Aries or Gemini, and the transit influence of Mars over it would be effective whenever

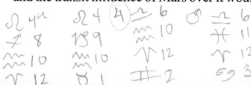

Mars transits from zero degrees to 10 degrees in Libra, Pisces, Aries or Cancer. However, once the longitude of the transit Jupiter or the transit Mars is 5 degrees, the transit influence would start separating and tapering down but it will clear the affliction only when their longitude is over ten degrees, assuming they are in direct movement. The orb of affliction for a non-mooltrikona house is five degrees on either side of the most effective point. We hope the readers are able to understand this dimension for better analysis.

Measuring Strength of the Houses

In case a mooltrikona sign falls in a house, the strength of the house is gauged through the strength of the lord and the nature of the conjunctions/aspects to the most effective point of the house. In the case of non-mooltrikona signs, the strength of the house is gauged only through the nature of the conjunctions/aspects to its most effective point. You will find in your experience that until and unless there is a close influence of a functional malefic planet on the most effective point of a house, the significations of the house containing a non-mooltrikona sign will not bother the person, at all. That is to say that the person will not seek astral consultation or remedies for the significations of the unafflicted houses containing a non-mooltrikona sign. The rising degree in the ascendant is known as the most effective point of all the houses.

Strong Planets

A strong natal planet protects and promotes its general significations and the significations of its mooltrikona house. Any planet is considered strong when its longitude is within 5 to 25 degrees and it is not in the state of weakness. It can increase its strength if:

a) it occupies own or good navamsa and other divisions.

b) it is under the close influence of functional benefic planets.

c) it occupies its exaltation, mooltrikona sign.

d)   it is placed in the Sun-like houses, that is the second, third and ninth houses.

Any planet has capacity to bless the person with its results if its natal strength is at least 60% and it is unafflicted. In such a situation the results may come with some delay and of slightly lower order. With the help of the strengthening measures - gemstones or a Special Power Kavach - the strength of the planets, where it is less than 60%, can be brought to the level of 60% so that it blesses the person with the significations ruled by it.

One can strengthen the weak planets (i) by way of a Kavach if the planetary strength is between 50% to 60%; (ii) by way of a special power Kavach if the planetary strength is between 35% to 50%; and (iii) by way of a special purpose Kavach with gemstones if the planetary strength is lower than 35%.

Weak Planets

A weak natal planet is not capable of fully protecting/ promoting its general significations and the significations of its mooltrikona house during the course of its sub-periods and during the triple transit functional malefic influences. A planet becomes weak when:

1)   The most effective point of its mooltrikona sign is afflicted by a functional malefic planet within an orb of one degree.

2)   The most effective point of its house of placement is afflicted by a functional malefic planet, within an orb of one degree for mooltrikona signs or within an orb of five degrees for non-mooltrikona signs.

3)   It is conjunct or aspected by any functional malefic planet within an orb of one degree.

4)   It is combust due to its nearness to the Sun.

5)   It occupies malefic houses from the ascendant, except if it is in its own mooltrikona sign.

6) It occupies its sign of debilitation.

7) It is in infancy or old-age.

8) It occupies its debilitated sign in navamsa.

9) It occupies the mooltrikona sign of a weak planet. However, its strength would be equal to the strength of its ultimate dispositor.

In case of special or multiple afflictions, the otherwise "strong" planet is considered afflicted (and weak) even when the orb of affliction is of two degrees.

The affliction is special or multiple i.e. when it comes from:

1) a conjunction with/ aspect from the most malefic planet,

2) an aspect from a functional malefic planet placed in a dusthana,

3) a conjunction with Rahu or Ketu (Rahu-Ketu axis),

4) an aspect of a functional malefic planet afflicted by other(s) functional malefic planet,

5) more than one functional malefic planet at the same time,

Fairly strong planet: A planet which has at least 70% power, is unafflicted and well placed, is considered as fairly strong planet.

Mild affliction: An affliction to the extent of 25% or less to a strong or fairly strong planet or the most effective point of a non-mooltrikona sign house is considered as a mild affliction. **The quantitative strength analysis for the planets can be obtained with the help of the following insights:**

a) A planet will lose strength to the extent of 75% if its mooltrikona sign house is afflicted.

b) A weak planet placed in an afflicted house will lose strength to the extent of 75%.

c) An otherwise strong planet placed in a non mooltrikona sign afflicted house will lose strength to the extent of 50%. Such a planet may give good results in the first place and will cause setbacks later.

d) A closely afflicted weak planet will lose strength to the extent of 75%.

e) A closely afflicted otherwise strong planet will lose strength to the extent of 50%. Such a planet will give good results in the first place and will cause setbacks later.

f) A planet becoming weak due to close combustion will lose strength to the extent of 75% if the Sun is a functional malefic planet. Where the Sun is a functional benefic and it causes combustion to another planet, the planet will become 50% weak for the purpose of transit affliction. A combust planet in its sign of debilitation and placed in a malefic house will have only 10% power.

g) When planets are placed in the malefic houses, they generally lose strength by 50% besides suffering through the significations of the malefic house. The placement in the sixth house can involve the person in disputes, debts and can cause ill health. The placement in the eighth house can cause serious obstructions for the significations ruled by the planet. The placement in the twelfth house can cause expenses and losses for the significations of the planet.

h) When planets are placed in their signs of debilitation, they lose strength by 50%. When planets are placed in their signs of debilitation in birth chart and navamsa, they lose strength by 75%.

i) If in Rasi chart the planet is badly placed and at the same time debilitated in navamsa it would lose strength to the extent of 60%.

j) A badly placed planet in its sign of debilitation will lose its power by 75%.

k) A planet debilitated in navamsa would lose power by 25%.

When the lord of the sixth house is in the ascendant the person gets involved in controversies. Discussing such a person also breeds controversies.

Sun-Like Planets

The second house rules status of the person in the society or with the Government. The third house rules the communication power of the person which is an important aspect for leadership. The ninth house is the house of fortune and rules happiness from father and preceptor. The lords of the second, third and ninth houses, wherever other than the Sun, act like the Sun for the various ascendants:

Ascendant	Sun Like Planets
1. Aries	Jupiter
2. Taurus	The Moon
3. Gemini	The Moon and Saturn
4. Cancer	Mercury
5. Leo	Mercury, Venus and Mars
6. Virgo	Venus
7. Libra	Jupiter
8. Scorpio	Jupiter and the Moon
9. Sagittarius	Saturn
10. Capricorn	Saturn and Mercury
11. Aquarius	Mars and Venus
12. Pisces	Mars

Any planet placed in the sign Leo has comparatively more power and certainly up by 25% than the actual power of the said planet(s).

When being the lord of the second house a Sun-like planet is placed in Leo sign it gains additional strength.

When the Sun itself is placed in a Sun-like house, it also gains 25% additional strength. In case the Sun is a functional malefic planet when placed in a Sun like house, it should not afflict the house to gain the additional strength.

If the Leo sign is in a malefic house and the Sun is placed in this house, the bad placement of the Sun would not be applicable and the Sun would be strong if not in infancy, old age or debilitated in navamsa.

Let us take an example for understanding the calculation of the strength of the Sun-like planets. Suppose Libra is rising with 22.4 deg. The Sun is placed in the fourth House, close to the MEP and unafflicted. It is not in old age. The MEP of the eleventh house is also unafflicted. This Sun would be strong but not having any additional strength.

Suppose Aries is rising and if Jupiter is in 9th House (Sun-like) in its own mooltrikona sign but in infancy (2.5 deg) and Jupiter is unafflicted, then its strength would be 50% + 25% increase for its being a Sun- like planet which is equal to 62.5%. If Jupiter is placed in another Sun -Like house, its strength will have a further rise of 25%. A planet by being lord of a Sun- like house and by being placed in another Sun -Like house can achieve the strength up to 100% in commensuration to its weakness due to infancy or old age.

In the case of Sun-like planets, the lord of the second house gets the first place, the lord of the third house gets the second place and the lord of the ninth house gets third place in importance.

Significators: In addition to ruling the houses containing their mooltrikona signs, the planets also act as Karakas (significators) for various houses. The various planets act as significators for the houses indicated against each:

Planet	Houses
The Sun	First, second, ninth and tenth houses
The Moon	Fourth house
Mars	Third and tenth houses
Mercury	Sixth and tenth houses
Jupiter	Second, fifth, ninth and eleventh houses
Venus	Fourth, seventh and twelfth houses
Saturn	Ayushkaraka (longevity) i.e. the eighth house

When strong, the various planets act as secondary significators for the following houses/matters:

Planet	House/Matter
The Sun	Fifth house, digestion, heart, leadership, job
The Moon	Tenth house/Public relations
Mars	First house/Energy
	Fourth house/Real estate
	Sixth house/Health
Mercury	Second house/Speech
	Third house/Communication ability
	Sixth house/Health
Jupiter	Ninth house/Spiritual fulfilment
Venus	Twelfth house/Happy married life and comforts
Saturn	Eleventh house/Easy income

Weak Signs

The signs Cancer and Virgo are considered weak signs. This is because the planets Moon and Mercury remain weak in transit and they bring down the strength of the planets placed in the Cancer and Virgo signs. When the Moon and or Mercury are placed in these signs they become more weak.

Rahu-Like Planets

The mooltrikona sign lords of the eighth and twelfth houses act as Rahu-like planets. The Rahu-like planets give inclinations for greed, over ambitiousness, encroachments, materialistic pursuits, lust, obstructions, mishaps and loss of patience.

Where there is no mooltrikona sign in the sixth house, afflicting Ketu acts as sixth lord being significator for injuries, financial constraints and losses through disputes.

Results of Exchange of Houses or Asterisms

In classical works the situation, in which a planet 'A' is placed in a sign or nakshatra ruled by the planet 'B' and the planet 'B' is placed in a sign or nakshatra ruled by the planet 'A', is considered as exchange of houses or exchange of nakshatra (asterisms). For example, if the Sun is placed in the sign Scorpio and the planet Mars is placed in the sign, Leo, then the classical works consider this as exchange of houses by the Sun and Mars.

Under the Systems' Approach, we do not recognize this concept. Each planet is considered, separately, for its placement, strength, relationship with other planets, etc.

Triple Transit Triggering Influence

The significant events are triggered by the interplay of the relationship between transit planets and natal planets/MEPs. The results generated depend upon the significations ruled by the planets involved, the significations ruled by their mooltrikona houses, the significations ruled by their houses of placement, either natally or in transit, and/or the significations ruled by the natal house(s) whose MEPs are under transit impact. This is called the triple transit triggering influence (TTT) as it is true for the three possible combinations of transit influence i.e. transit over natal, transit over transit, and natal over transit. In other words:

1) Whenever any weak natal planet/MEP is transited by FM(s), it triggers a significant undesirable incident concerning that weak natal planet or that weak house, whichever is the case. This is more so when the weak natal planet or the lord/ significator of the weak house is weak in transit too.

2) Whenever any strong natal planet/MEP is transited by FM(s), it triggers a mild unfavorable incident concerning that strong natal planet or that strong house, whichever is the case.

3) Whenever any weak natal FB/MEP is transited by FB(s), it triggers hopes or non-significant happy incidents concerning that planet or house, whichever is the case.

4) Whenever any strong natal FB/MEP is transited by FB(s), it triggers significant happy incidents concerning that planet or house, whichever is the case. This is more so when the planet or the lord/significator of the house is strong in transit too.

5) Whenever planets in transit form close conjunctions amongst themselves, the happenings occur depending upon their functional nature in connection with the houses with reference to a particular ascendant.

6) If the close conjunction or aspect(s) of planets in transit involve two or more FBs with reference to a particular ascendant, it triggers happy events pertaining to all these planets.

7) If one of the planets involved in close conjunction or aspect in a transit planetary movement is a FM, it harms the significations of the other FB(s) involved with reference to a particular ascendant.

8) If both or all the planets forming close conjunction in transit with reference to a particular ascendant are FMs, it harms the significations of all the planets involved.

9) Whenever any weak transit planet forms close conjunction with or become closely aspected by natal FM(s), it triggers a significant undesirable incident concerning that weak transit planet. This is more so when the planet is weak in rasi too.

10) Whenever any strong transit planet forms close conjunction with or becomes closely aspected by natal FM(s), it triggers a mild unfavorable incident concerning that strong transit planet.

11) Whenever any weak transit FB forms close conjunction with or become closely aspected by natal FB(s), it triggers hopes or non-significant happy incidents pertaining to that weak transit planet.

12) Whenever any strong transit FB forms close conjunction with or become closely aspected by natal FB(s), it triggers significant happy incidents pertaining to that strong transit planet. This is more so when the planet is strong in rasi too.

13) The transit effects are always seen with reference to the natal ascendant.

14) In setting the trends, the sub-period lord has maximum say. However, the transit impacts mentioned above supersede the trend results of the sub-period lord.

15) The malefic transit impact of slow moving FMs like Jupiter, Saturn, Rahu and Ketu is more pronounced when, during the course of their close conjunctions/aspects, they move slower as compared to their normal speed or become stationary. This is true both for natal and transit influences.

16) During the sub-periods of the FBs, the transit impacts of FBs are stronger while transit impacts of FMs are mild. If the sub-period lord is strong, then the transit influences of FBs cause significant happy events.

17) During the sub-periods of FMs, the transit impacts of FBs are mild while the transit impacts of FMs are more severe. If the transit influences are from strong FBs, then the benefic results may be comparatively better but with some delay.

18) The duration of the transit results ceases to exist as soon as the transit close conjunction or aspect separates. The orb of separation as explained earlier would depend upon the strength

of the planets on which the transit influences have been created.

19) Whenever a transiting FM transits the MEP of any house, it afflicts that house as well as the aspected house(s). A transit FM never afflicts its own mooltrikona house, except when the functional malefic planet is already afflicted and/or afflicts from a dusthana/malefic house.

20) A transit FM will always afflict its natal position by conjunction or aspect, except when natally placed in its own mooltrikona house.

21) A natal FM will always afflict its transit position by aspect even when transiting its own mooltrikona house.

22) A natal FM will always afflict its transit position by conjunction, except when placed in its own mooltrikona house.

The triple transit triggering influence will help you in understanding the impact of planetary influences more precisely. For further detailed study the interested readers may study the book, Triple Transit Influence of Planets.

Relative Importance of Planetary Influences

Regarding afflictions, we can have:

1) Afflictions in rasi/natal chart.

2) Afflictions of transit on rasi.

3) Afflictions of transit on transit.

4) Afflictions of rasi on transit.

Afflictions in Rasi, being permanent afflictions, are more serious as they will manifest during all life as malefic tendencies present whenever the sub-periods of related planets are operating. They depend on the strength of the afflicted planets and the number/ proximity/maleficness of the afflictors. In the last three cases, as they are temporary afflictions, their degree of importance depend more on the lack of strength of the afflicted planets, the number/ duration of the afflictions, the proximity/maleficness of the afflictors, and the ruling sub-period in each case. The last one, afflictions of rasi on transit, are even more important than the other two for all the ascendants containing fast moving planets as functional malefic planets i.e. almost all: Aries (Mercury), Taurus (Venus, Mars), Leo (the Moon), Virgo (the Sun, Mars), Libra (Mercury), Scorpio (Venus, Mars), Sagittarius (the Moon), Capricorn (the Sun), Aquarius (the Moon, Mercury) and Pisces (the Sun, Venus, Mars). These fast moving functional malefic planets, that in the previous two conditions are not so problematic, create here serious problems whenever a slow planet in transit comes under their malefic influence. Unless astral remedies are earnestly performed, the problems may come up whenever the planet is weak and afflicted in any of these three transit conditions. The probability increases with the number of the transit conditions involved. The same reasoning applies to the triple transit triggering influences of functional benefic planets.

Regarding how to get the actual strengths of planets for a certain person at a specific time, the different kinds of strengths are:

1)   Strengths of planets in rasi/natal chart.

2)   Strengths of planets in transit.

3)   Strengths of planets in rasi modified by the aspects from transits.

4)   Strengths of planets in transit modified by the aspects from rasi.

The strength of planets in rasi is the most important. The last three conditions help and become more pertinent if condition 1) exists. If planets in rasi are weak, they will temporarily become strong only a little by the existence of the last three conditions if no strengthening measures have been used.

Exalted Functional Malefic Planets

Exalted planets if functional malefic planets and at the same time afflicting by close conjunction or aspect other weak planet(s) or the most effective point of the house(s) do cause sufferings with regard to the significations ruled by the said afflicted planet(s) or house(s). The exalted planets, when badly placed, become weak and afflicted.

Role of Planets

A planet plays its role in the following manner:

a)   As a natural significator for various things.

b)   As a lord of the house containing its mooltrikona sign to protect and promote the significations of that house depending upon its natal strength.

c)   Through its relationship with other planetary configurations in a birth chart.

The strength of a planet governs the role of that planet for (a) and (b) above in protecting and promoting its general and particular significations. The functional nature of the planet governs its role as at (c) above.

Analyzing Results of Sub-Period Lords

Events fructify in the sub-periods of planets. Therefore, it is very important that we understand the method of analyzing the dasa (main period) and bhukti (sub-period) results. The results of the general significations of the sub-period lord depend upon its strength, placement, conjunction and aspects to the same. The significations of the house of placement are touched when transit planets create benefic or malefic influences on the sub-period lord, depending upon their functional nature whether benefic or malefic. In the sub-period of a planet, the following significations are touched:

1) The general significations of the planet. For example the Sun rules father, social status, position with the government, male child, digestive system, heart, blood pressure, etc.

2) The significations of the house where the mooltrikona sign of the said planet is placed. In case in the mooltrikona house some functional malefic planet is placed close to the most effective point, or some functional malefic planet is closely aspecting the most effective point of the said house, or some planet is closely afflicted then during the sub-periods of the afflicting and afflicted planet(s) the significations of the mooltrikona house shall not prosper and shall face problems indicated by the afflicting planet depending upon its lordship. A natal/transit functional malefic planet never afflicts its own mooltrikona house, except when the functional malefic planet is already afflicted and/or afflicts from a dusthana/malefic house.

3) The significations of the houses where the planet is placed.

4) During the sub-period of a planet all the impacts on the house, which contains the mooltrikona sign of the said planet, also come into force. Due to such influences on the most effective point by a strong functional benefic planet even the sub-period of a weak planet would be blessing the person with good or very good results. Similarly, a close impact of a functional malefic planet on the most effective point of a mooltrikona house may not allow the planet ruling that mooltrikona house to show good results in its sub-periods even if the said planet is strong in the natal chart.

Let us see the application of most malefic planet and most effective point while analyzing the results of sub-periods, with the help of an example.

Example Chart 4

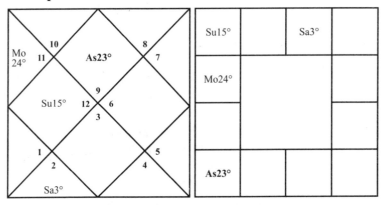

The 23 degree of Sagittarius rises in the ascendant. Therefore, the most effective point of all the houses will be 23 degree. Any planet conjunct within 5 degrees on either side i.e. within 18 degrees to 28 degrees in any house would be influencing the significations of the house in question in a pronounced manner depending upon the functional nature of that planet. The Moon is placed at 24 degrees in the third house in the sign Aquarius ruled by Saturn. As the Moon is the most malefic planet, this placement afflicts simultaneously the most effective point of the third and ninth houses, weakening their respective lords and itself. Since the Moon is conjunct with the most effective point of the third house, it not only destroys the initiatives of the person but during the sub-periods of both the Moon and Saturn it will not allow any ventures/initiatives of the person to succeed. The aspect of the Moon to the most effective point to the ninth house would also cause obstructions to the significations of the ninth house during the sub-periods of both the Sun and the Moon. The Sun is lord of the ninth house while the Moon is aspecting and malefically influencing the ninth house. In such cases if the weak Sun is well placed as in this case, the impact of the influence of the Moon would be a little bit milder than if the Sun is badly placed. As Saturn is very weak due to infancy, bad placement and the exact affliction of the most malefic planet on the most effective point of its mooltrikona house, during the sub-periods of the Moon and Saturn the impact would be quite grave.

Impact of Transit

The impact of transit functional malefic planets is on both the functional malefic planets and the functional benefic planets. The things governed by the planets would be their general and particular significations. Similarly, when the impact is on the most effective point of a house the significations of the house occupied and the house(s) aspected, both mooltrikona and non-mooltrikona houses would be influenced by the transit planet.

Transit of planets over the natal position of functional malefic planets or close aspect of natal functional malefic planets on planets in transit also spoil the significations of the planets in transit. By transit strength we mean the planet should be strong in transit.

Interaction Between the Sub-Periods and Transit

During the course of the sub-period of a planet the significations of the mooltrikona house ruled by the sub-period lord, the general significations of the planet and the significations of the house where the planet is placed would be touched.

The transit means when the planetary position on any given date subsequent to the date of the birth is studied with reference to the ascendant and the position of the planets in the natal chart.

For example, let us take a chart with the sign Sagittarius rising in the ascendant. In this chart the lord of the eleventh house, Venus, is placed in the twelfth house, ruling losses. During the sub-period of Venus trouble to elder brother, loss of income and trouble to friends is indicated. To cause a death-like event or some serious trouble to the elder brother the transit functional malefic planets

Rahu/Ketu may form close conjunction or aspect with any of the three positions:

i)   Most effective point of the eleventh house.

ii) Natal position of the sub-period lord, Venus.

iii) Transit position of the sub-period lord, Venus.

The conjunction or aspect of natal Moon, Rahu or Ketu with transit Venus may also cause the same fatality if the natal Venus is weak.

Example Chart 5

The example chart pertains to a lady born 22nd December 1964, at 0850 hrs at Copenhagen, Denmark 55N41' 12E'35 CE TIME (GMT + 1).

In her case Venus main period (dasa) Venus sub-period (bhukti) started on 30th Oct 1981 and was to run up to 1st March 1985. Now from the horoscope we would see that an incident like loss of an elder brother is seen in the sub-period of Venus as Venus ruling the elder brother is placed in the house of losses. The transit Venus was of 1 degree in the sign Capricorn on 2nd February 1982. It apparently retrograded and came into contact with transit Ketu at 29 degrees in the sign Sagittarius on the 7th February 1982. Up to the 21st February 1982, the transit Venus and transit Ketu were within 3 degrees range. The sub-period lord was not only weak due to its being in infancy but it was also in close conjunction with Ketu. Being placed in the house of losses in the natal chart Ketu is having the inclinations of causing loss with whatever planet it forms close conjunction or aspect with. The person lost her elder brother.

The sub-period lord sets the trend according to its lordship, placement and other natal influences on itself in rasi while the transit/natal planets cause influence whenever they come into contact with the natal/transit position of the sub-period lord.

We hope this gives better understanding into the interaction between the transit results and the sub-period lord results with the help of the above example.

Reliability of Treating a House as Ascendant for Signified Relationship

We cannot treat a house as ascendant for the relation signified by that house. For example, ninth house for father and the seventh house for wife, etc. We can't decipher educational prospects of father, his assets, etc. from the twelfth house which is the fourth house from the ninth house. The status of father in general can be seen from the Sun and the ninth house. The detailed analysis of any relation can only be made from his/her own horoscope. Regarding spouse, children, parents, elder/younger siblings and friends only general indications can be seen from the person's chart. For example, from the person's chart we can see whether the person will derive happiness from his/her children or at a particular time whether the child is enjoying or in trouble but we cannot identify in detail about the educational, professional or emotional matters of a child.

Measuring Capacity of Planets

While studying the impact of a planet, depending upon its strength, during the course of its sub-period both the natal and transit positions of the planet under operation are to be studied.

The result of a particular house will be influenced by a transiting planet when it is near to its most effective point depending upon its functional nature whether benefic or malefic.

A weak planet, too, has the capacity to protect its house if it is well placed, unafflicted, under the beneficial influence of functional benefic planets through close aspect/conjunction or aspects its own mooltrikona house.

Bright Rays

A planet with bright rays means a non-combust planet.

Measuring Strength of Planets in Infancy/Old Age

The results of the planets in infancy or old age vary in degree of strength as per their longitudes as detailed below:

Infancy
When 0 degree power is zero

When 1 degree power is 20%

When 2 degrees power is 40%

When 3 degrees power is 60%

When 4 degrees power is 80%

When 5 degrees power is 100%

Old Age

When 30 degrees power is zero

When 29 degrees power is 20%

When 28 degrees power is 40%

When 27 degrees power is 60%

When 26 degrees power is 80%

When 25 degrees power is 100%

Exaltation sign adds to the strength. The peak point of exaltation or debilitation has very little relevance.

Divisional Charts

The divisional charts are the charts which are drawn by division of houses for specialized analysis of a particular signification; for example navamsa for considering general fortune and marriage, etc., and dasamsa for considering professional aspects in a birth chart. For a detailed study on this subject, you can read the author's book, "How to Study Divisional Charts".

Chalit Chakra

This is a redundant concept so far as the Systems' Approach is concerned. The Systems' Approach identifies the functional nature of the planets on the basis of the ascendant. Each planet is treated in the house in which it is placed. A planet placed in the eighth house going to seventh or ninth house as per chalit chakra can never give good results. Its periods will bestow weak results because of the position of the planet being weak due to its bad placement and there will be obstructions and mishaps. The astrologers, who consider chalit chakra, fail in their predictions.

Evolution of the Soul

The evolution of the soul depends on the strength of the Sun, Jupiter and the lords of the tenth and first houses.

Measuring Afflictions

The quantum of influence of the functional malefic planet (FM) on another planet or most effective point (MEP) of the house is gauged through the closeness of the conjunction or aspect. The afflictions to the planets/houses are caused by the close conjunction or aspect of the FMs in a birth chart. Regarding otherwise "strong" planets and/or MT houses, the normal afflictions are effective within one degree range while the special/multiple afflictions are effective within two degrees range, making these otherwise "strong" planets/ MT houses weak on this account. The normal afflictions to weak planets/MT houses are fully effective if they are within one degree range while afflictions are 80%, 60%, 40%, 20% and 0% if the afflicting planet is having a 1 deg, 2 deg, 3 deg, 4 deg and 5 deg longitudinal difference, respectively, from the weak planet/MEP of the weak MT house. The special/multiple afflictions to weak planets/MT houses are fully effective if they are within two degrees range while afflictions are 75%, 50%, 25% and 0% if the afflicting planet(s) is having a 2 deg, 3 deg, 4 deg and 5 deg longitudinal difference, respectively, from the weak planet/MEP of the weak MT house. It is most severe if the weak and afflicted planets are badly placed. The experience based on the feedback of the people indicates that these afflictions can be taken care of up to 80 - 90% with the help of the astral remedies i.e. Kavach, gemstones and charities, etc. If the planets/houses are strong, the damage is least. For non-MT houses, the impact of the affliction is 100% to 0% depending upon the longitudinal difference between the FM and MEP of the house as explained above for the weak planets/MT houses. If a planet being lord of a house is weak then one should see the strength of the significator (karaka) and the supplementary houses as well.

Impact of Transit Exalted Rahu and Ketu

The impact of well placed exalted Rahu over the well placed strong functional benefic planets is good for materialistic prosperity. The transit over the weak functional benefic planets gives small gains or creates false hopes. The transit over the functional malefic planets causes anxiety and delays with regard to the significations of the houses where the mooltrikona sign of the functional malefic planet under transit is placed. The impact of the transit of well placed exalted Ketu will be bad only on weak and afflicted planets when Ketu in transit is stationary.

When in dusthana houses the results of exalted Rahu/Ketu are as under:

a)   When in the sixth house, it gives losses through theft and fire, debts, cheating and expenses on treatment of illness. If the lord of the sixth house is strong, Rahu can give some financial gains through manipulations.

(b) When in the eighth house, it can give inheritance, obstructions, manipulating tendencies and increased tendencies for sensual pleasures.

c)   When in the twelfth house, it can give bad health, loss of sleep, craving for excessive gratification of senses, visits to far-off places or foreign lands.

Impact of Combust Planets

When the Sun is a functional benefic planet its conjunction with other well placed functional benefic planets is good and gives exponential growth for the significations of the planets in close conjunction with the Sun. The combust planets suffer under the triple transit influences of functional malefic planets. This can, however, be guarded by application of the strengthening and propitiating astral remedies, to a large extent.

When the Sun is a functional malefic planet or a functional malefic planet or planets are closely and mutually influencing the Sun, the significations of all the planets involved suffer in their sub-periods as also during transit impacts. If a malefic planet is close to the Sun, it hurts the Sun. It affects the Sun. The malefic planet also gets combust and becomes weak.

For example see the following chart:

Example Chart 6

		Ju20° Ra3°	
Sa15°			Mo10°
			As16°
Ke3°	Su15° Ve18° Me13°	Ma21°	

All the three planets in the third house are in close conjunction amongst themselves and the conjunction is good except the transit afflictions which will be short-lived if the influencing Rahu and Ketu during the transit do not become stationary. In this chart, the sub-periods of Venus, the Sun and Mercury in the main periods of the functional benefic planets will give good initiatives, increased income and happiness, involvement in writing, artistic pursuits, and status rise through such activities.

Impact of Retrograde Planets in Astrology

The planets are always moving. When we see the record of movement of planets in the zodiac from the ephemeris, we find that the planets move forward. Sometimes, planets appear to be moving back due to the relative position and motion of planets. When a planet instead of moving forward appears to be moving backwards in the zodiac, it is called retrograde. All planets, other than the Sun and the Moon, appear to be moving backward on different occasions. Rahu and Ketu generally seem to move backward.

This is only a visionary phenomenon as this occurs due to different speeds of the planets in relation to the earth. The effects on a natal chart are due to fixed angular position of planets with reference to a particular place on the earth for a particular time, natal or transit.

Though the classical as well as some of the modern commentators have ascribed different views for the results of retrograde planets, the authors are of the firm view that retrograde planets are to be treated in a normal way as per their longitudes, so far as the natal planetary influences are concerned in a horoscope. However, the transit influences of a planet appearing to be in retrograde motion and then direct motion are prolonged on a specified degree(s).

However, for understanding the impact of a transit retrograde planet it is necessary that one learns predictive techniques and methodology for reading the triple transit influences.

Impact of Planetary Combinations (Yoga)

The planetary combinations (yoga) in a horoscope are generated through close conjunctions, close aspects and placements of planets. When two or more functional benefic planets form close relationship among themselves or with the most effective points of benefic houses, they generate good results related to their mooltrikona houses. This type of relationship caused due to the close conjunction/aspect is known as an auspicious yoga. If two functional malefic planets form a close relationship, they cause an inauspicious yoga and destroy the results related to their mooltrikona houses. If one functional benefic planet and one functional malefic planet form a close relationship, this causes an inauspicious yoga that destroys the results of the mooltrikona house ruled by the functional benefic planet. When a functional benefic planet occupies a malefic house, this causes yoga for misfortune related to the significations of its mooltrikona house. Similarly, when a functional malefic planet closely influences the most effective point of a house, it destroys the significations of that house, except if it is its own mooltrikona house.

The impact of Rajyoga or Dhanayoga accrues only if the planets involved are strong. Whenever, the planets ruling benefic houses conjoin or mutually aspect closely, they form good yoga (say Rajyoga) connected with the indications of both the houses involved, provided they are strong. The involvement of a planet ruling the house of income and/or wealth produces a Dhanayoga. In other words, mere location of a planet or a set of planets in a particular sign or house without creating a close relationship through a close conjunction or aspect does not result into any yoga. The planets involved in Rajyoga bless the person with name, fame, wealth, comforts, etc., during their sub-periods.

Similarly, until and unless any functional malefic planet forms a close conjunction or aspect with other planet(s) or house(s) they do not produce any Duryoga or even Kalsarpa yoga. The misnomer Kalsarpa yoga is being propagated by those persons who have failed to correctly identify the functional nature of planets in various nativities and have not been able to pin point the reasons for miseries. Any chart containing the so-called Kalsarpa yoga will not give bad results until and unless Rahu-Ketu or other functional malefic planets cause severe conjunctions or aspects with weak planets or houses in that particular birth chart. Under the Systems' Approach, the analysis is always done with reference to the placement of planets, their strength and weaknesses and their mutual relationship with reference to the ascendant and its most effective point in particular. The planets involved in Duryogas cause miseries/ tragedies as per their nature depending upon their lordships, during their sub-periods.

Another misnomer, 'Neechbhanga Rajyoga' is not coming from the propounding father but has found its place in the subsequent classical commentaries like Phaladipika, etc. The Systems' Approach does not believe in this concept and treats the debilitated planet as a weak planet.

How to Proceed with Analysis for Identifying the Problem Areas

For starting analysis, underline the functional malefic planets. Study the strength of the planets and identify the exact or close conjunctions/aspects. See also if any special/multiple affliction exits. Put a circle around the planets/houses which are afflicted. Now you can start the analysis.

The long-term problem is always with regard to the weak and afflicted planets or the sub-periods of the functional malefic planets in the natal chart. The short-term problem is indicated by the (i) transit of functional malefic(s) over the natal planets, (ii) when transit planets come under the influence of natal functional malefic planets; and (iii) the close afflictions or bad placements of transit planets with reference to a particular ascendant. The good results should be indicated for the significations of the strong functional benefic planets having close benefic conjunctions/aspects.

The position of functional benefic planet(s) in dusthanas or malefic houses make them weak and afflicted but if they aspect the most effective point of the house containing their own mooltrikona sign then despite weakness they are able to protect the significations of their mooltrikona house to some extent. Also, if they are placed in the eighth house near the most effective point of the house then despite weakness it is good as they aspect the most effective point of the second house. In the case of a functional benefic Mars, Jupiter or Saturn posited in the eighth house they also aspect two other houses besides the second house.

The case studies included in all our books bring out the techniques for quickly spotting the prominent events in life. For detailed study of the divisional charts, the readers may refer to our book, "How to Study Divisional Charts".

Insights

Fairly strong planet: A planet which has at lest 70% power, is unafflicted and well placed, is considered as fairly strong planet.

Mild affliction: An affliction to the extent of 25% or less to a strong or fairly strong planet or the most effective point of a non-mooltrikona sign house is considered as a mild affliction.

Whenever Rahu-Ketu axis is placed exactly over the most effective points of houses containing odd signs besides afflicting the houses occupied and aspected, it turns the planets Saturn, the Sun, Venus, Mars and Jupiter weak by afflicting their mooltrikona houses.

Whenever Rahu-Ketu axis is placed exactly over the most effective points of houses containing even signs besides afflicting the houses occupied and aspected, it turns the planets the Moon and Mercury weak by afflicting their mooltrikona houses.

The close influence of the lord of the eighth house or Rahu or the lord of the twelfth house on the lord of the seventh house, and/ or the most effective point of the seventh house and/or Venus and the close influence of Rahu on the lord of the eighth house gives indulgence out of marital bond for excessive sensual pleasures and endangers the person with sexually transmitted diseases.

The close affliction of the nodes to weak planets makes one vulnerable to cancerous diseases. Ever since the author, V. K. Choudhry identified this planetary configuration giving cancerous results in the year 1989, our team had been very particular in watching the horoscopes with such planetary configuration for administering preventive astral remedies and we are very proud to say that in cases where the person had not started suffering from such a fatal disease, the preventive astral remedies proved to be of great help and the persons suspected for cancerous disease did not suffer in the sub-periods of such afflicting/afflicted planets.

A planet placed in the mooltrikona sign cannot exceed the strength of its dispositor.

During the sub period of a planet the results of planets placed in its mooltrikona sign fructify simultaneously.

Prediction of unfavorable results can be/is made for the significations ruled by the weak planets even if there are no afflictions in the natal chart and no planet is badly placed. A strong planet will give beneficial results of its general and particular significations throughout the life. If it is away from the MEP of the house of its placement, it may give results for the significations of the said house in the later part of life.

An FM planet does not afflict its own MT sign by conjunction or by aspect. An FM planet will afflict its own MT sign by aspect only if it itself is afflicted by another FM planet. Dispositor weakness or bad placement affliction is not applicable in this case. The benefit of aspect to the MT sign of FM is limited to the proportion of the strength of the FM.

The third house also rules learning, comprehension, vitality, leadership, vision and success.

The placement of the tenth lord in the second house gives professional education.

The strength of Sun or the Sun like houses or planets improve the results of other planets to some extent.

The strong affliction of MMP to the significators of longevity, the placement of planets in the 8th house and the afflicted Moon cause short life span.

Close afflictions to MEP of the houses harm the main significations of the house.

The strong planets give results without much efforts while the weak planets need more efforts with little/delayed success.

Give due consideration to placement of the planets. The planets placed in the third house take the person to MBA / marketing like studies. The strong planets bring brilliance coupled with stability. The weak planets show their impact through instability.

The affliction depends upon the closeness of the functional malefic planet to the planet/house which is being afflicted.

The afflicting power of the functional malefic planet does not reduce due to its weakness. The afflicting power of the functional malefic planet increases when it is placed in a malefic house or it itself is under affliction.

If the planet/house under affliction is weak, the impact of affliction will be more.

For strong planet the orb of affliction is one degree.

The orb of affliction is two degrees for strong planets in the following cases:

-       multiple affliction;

-       affliction by the most malefic planet;

-       affliction by Rahu and Ketu both;

-       affliction from a planet afflicted by other functional malefic planet;

-       affliction from a planet placed in dusthana (malefic house),

For weak planets/houses the orb of affliction is five degrees.

The affliction to the MEP of houses is more severe in comparison to the affliction to a planet.

The karma results arise through the principles of divine justice. Jyotish/Astral remedies are the means for alleviating the karma results.

The important tools for predictive accuracy are the functional nature of planets, strength of planets, inter-relationships of planets, divisional charts, impact of Rahu & Ketu, planetary periods and triple transit triggers.

For differentiating between

- having issues in a particular area throughout life

- enjoying good results in a particular area but in some sub-periods facing issues and drawbacks

The guiding principle is that the planets give results as per their strength in their sub periods. Transit influences take precedence over sub period results. The strong/exact afflictions to natal planets are not easy things to be dealt with. The continuous propitiation with strengthening of afflicted planets help. Some other strong planets in the birth chart help in bringing down the impact of strong afflictions. The strong planets, in general, give good results for their significations throughout the life. Where there are no strong or well placed planets, there is limited hope of things turning good. To answer questions for timing of events, see the natal and transit planetary strengths, operating sub period and transit to answer these questions. For example, in a query for job, if the natal determinants of profession and the Sun are strong or well placed with at least 60% power and there is no transit affliction the person is likely to get work in a couple of months' time. Another month or so can be added if Rahu-Ketu are stationary. For rest of the people it may take longer time and they need strengthening of their planets and propitiation of the planets causing afflictions.

Whenever there are double or multiple close/exact afflictions, these take first priority in giving their results. In case such close/exact afflictions of MMP and Rahu-Ketu axis are suffered by the prime significator of the marriage, the marriage can be delayed inordinately or even denied. In such cases the use of a special purpose Kavach and continuous special propitiatory remedies become absolutely essential.

Decade per degree rule: The impact of conjunctions and aspects is measured in terms of a decade per degree of closeness. If it is an exact aspect or conjunction between the two planets the impact is felt in the sub periods falling in the first ten years of life. If there is a close aspect or conjunction with a longitudinal difference of one to two degrees the impact is felt in the sub periods of the planets falling in the second decade. If there is a close aspect or conjunction with a longitudinal difference of two to three degrees the impact is felt in the sub periods of the planets falling in the third decade. If there is a close aspect or conjunction with a longitudinal difference of three to four degrees the impact is felt in the sub periods of the planets falling in the fourth decade. If there is a close aspect or conjunction with a longitudinal difference of four to five degrees the impact is felt in the sub periods of the planets falling in the fifth decade.

The results can be further influenced by stationary transit influence or the strength of the planets involved.

When any exalted functional malefic planet, other than Mercury, is conjunct with the MEP of the house of its placement, it becomes weak.

Strong Venus hastens marriage.

Strong Sun brings down the level of sufferings due to afflictions.

Metals ruled by planets: The Sun rules copper and gold. The Moon rules silver. Mars rules copper. Mercury rules brass. Jupiter rules gold. Venus rules silver and aluminum. Saturn rules iron, minerals and crude.

Planetary castes and Nature: Those with strong influence of Jupiter go in the learning, teaching, training, development and spiritual work - Brahmins. Those with strong Sun and Mars go for administrative / organization profession, government assignments & security forces are fighters - Kshatriyas. Those with strong Moon, Mercury and Venus go for trading / business ventures - vaishayas. Those with weak planets and strong influences of Saturn and Rahu go for routine jobs – Sudra.

While afflicting, the mooltrikona sign lords of the eighth and twelfth houses act as Rahu like planets.

The balance sheet of past lives is in the form of the birth chart. Purva punyas (good deeds of past lives) are seen from the IX house. Karma of this life (deeds of this life) are seen through the fifth and tenth houses. The strong planets represent the good Karma from past lives, while the weak planets and afflictions to planets and houses represent the bad karma brought forward. Afflictions point to very bad Karma, whereas weaknesses represent milder bad karma.

Vedic Astrology is an ancient universal knowledge on which we offer our views as other authors/astrologers have done in the past and are doing in the present.

The items for propitiation suggested are based on the planetary tastes mentioned in the Vedic literature and bhoota yagyam - one of the five great sacrifices. These have nothing to do with the remedies suggested in other books.

While we have expressed our views based on our experience, the readers are free for their own views and beliefs and for adopting the Systems' Approach brought out by us for interpreting the horoscopes.

The problems and mishaps are represented by the weak and weak and/or afflicted planets.

When the natal Moon is afflicted by Rahu, Rahu-like planets or is placed in the Rahu-like houses the person becomes more sensitive and especially to unfavorable incidents.

The exact affliction to badly placed lord of fourth or second or ninth or third house lord (most benefic planet) reduces the strength of other strong planets in the natal chart.

The weakness of the lord of the eighth house makes the father vulnerable to damage, both in terms of longevity and in terms of finances.

The weakness of the lord of the eighth house or fourth house curtails the financial resources or longevity of father. In Pisces ascendant there is no MT sign in the ninth and fourth houses. So, the eighth house becomes pertinent significator of the longevity of the father. We also consider the strength of the Sun in the natal chart as it is significator for father.

Affliction to the ascendant in any divisional chart by the eighth lord of the divisional chart is equally serious as the affliction to the prime determinants placed in eighth house of the divisional chart.

In divisional charts besides the affliction of R&K, the afflictions by the functional malefic planets of the divisional charts should be considered and the afflictions by the functional malefic planets of natal chart are not considered. Bad placements are also considered in the divisional charts.

The close influence of Rahu on the third lord makes the person adventurous.

The exact / close aspect of Rahu makes the person greedy and does not allow him/her to feel contented.

Suppose there is an exact conjunction/aspect of planets in the birth chart or there is an exact conjunction/aspect of a planet with the most effective point of a house in the birth chart. When this position of exact conjunction or aspect develops prolonged malefic transit influence the person faces multiple challenges in his/her life simultaneously.

The placement of planets is an important factor in horoscope reading. The placement of a planet gives results connected with the significations of the house ruled by the planet with the house of placement despite its weakness or despite the planet being away from the most effective point of the house. If a functional malefic planet is on the most effective point of a house it causes problems but the problems may be connected with the significations ruled by the said planet. If the lord of the second is placed in the twelfth house, the person may move to a distant place or a foreign land in connection with the professional status. If the second lord is placed in the tenth house the person may acquire status in life due to his/her professional achievements. If the second lord is placed in the fifth house, one may acquire professional qualification and acquire status through the same. If the second lord is placed in the seventh house one may attain status in a foreign land. If the second lord is placed in the fourth house one may attain status by being born in a resourceful family. If the second lord is placed in the eighth house one may attain status in life with some delay. If the second lord is placed in the ninth house one may be lucky to attain the status in life without much efforts with the help of parents and preceptor. If the second lord is placed in the eleventh house, one may acquire status in life because of good earnings in life and because of friendship with highly placed persons. If the second lord is placed in the second house, one may enjoy good status in life due to the appointment with the state or due to the family status. If the second lord is placed in the ascendant one may enjoy authoritative status.

The placement of the Sun and Mars in the third house brings courage. The close influence of the fifth lord on the tenth house brings the element of intellect. The placement of the planets in the second house, which rules status, brings status as per significations ruled by them. The good placement of eighth lord in the house of status brings easy gains with small or little efforts. The planets in the first house influence the personality traits. The planets in the second house contribute to professional ventures. The planets in the third house bring entrepreneurial ventures and opportunities. The planets in the fourth house contribute to assets. The planets in the fifth house contribute to learning. The planets in the sixth house involve the person in debts, health problems and conflicts. The planets placed in the seventh house give rise to living in foreign lands, long journeys and associations. The planets placed in the eighth house cause easy gains, obstructions and delays. The planets placed in the ninth house involve the person in family or religious traditions or spiritual pursuits. The planets placed in the tenth house involve the person in professions connected with the planet. The planets placed in the eleventh house contribute to earnings through the significations ruled by the concerned planets. The planets placed in the twelfth house take one to distant places and foreign lands and can cause losses and expenses.

During the sub period of Mercury things work with stresses and strains even when Mercury is strong and or well placed in the natal chart. This is due to the volatile strength of Mercury in transit. When Mercury is weak in the natal chart the results in its sub period do create stresses and strains. The situation becomes further difficult when either of the Sun or Mercury is a functional malefic planet.

Whenever the lord of the twelfth house is placed in the sixth house or afflicts some planet in the sixth house closely, there are chances of problems with government which may result in arrest, legal penalties, imprisonment, etc.

In case of transit of a planet in a malefic house, the impact starts from the day of entering into the malefic house and remains till it is out of the malefic house. It is important in case of slow moving planets. Patience and continued multiple peace making remedies help to a large extent. For example, if Saturn moves to sixth house one becomes vulnerable to disputes, diseases and debts for the entire period of stay of Saturn in the sixth house.

The close affliction to the Sun gives difficulties to the person, high blood pressure due to anxiety, difficulties to father / husband, child and makes the person vulnerable to severe infections / allergies.

The close affliction to the Moon gives difficulties to the person, difficulties to the mother, depressing thoughts, gynecology problems to ladies and immunity disorders.

Eclipses:

Eclipses, in general, does not make a strong or prolonged impact for living persons until and unless some slow moving planet is stationary or moving utterly slow or appearing retrograde near the degree of some natal planet in the chart of an individual or nation.

For those who are taking birth, there are chances that there are strong close afflictions to the Sun and/or the Moon or any other planet in the natal chart. This can certainly cause prolonged problems for the person.

SA is an all pervasive framework, touching upon all aspects of predictive astrology - both natal and mundane.

Caution: Astrologers do not have a television set and cannot give running commentary. The best thing is in the shortest possible time, indicate the strong and weak areas in chart and prescribe appropriate astral remedies. One acquires credentials or good reputation as an astrologer with one's competence over a period of time.

Chapter 2

Application of Astral Remedies

Medicine treats but Jyotish remedies prevent. The jyotish / astral remedies consist of a Kavach or a Special Power Kavach or a special purpose Kavach and the propitiatory astral remedies for the functional malefic planets. The application of astrological remedial measures is always advantageous in all aspects of life including health, education, profession and relationships. Astrology helps through predictions and astral remedies. Astrology enables wise people to charter and manage the course of success in life for health, career, love, relationships and financial matters. The interpretation and the effective jyotish remedies suggestion is based on the planetary influences in the individual horoscopes. Jyotish remedies act as panacea in all aspects of life and in harmony with medical remedies for various types of health problems. Jyotish remedies help in diagnosis of the health problems and application of medical remedies. The blessed ones are impelled by the divine forces for making use of the ultimate knowledge through application of jyotish remedies / astral remedies - both propitiating astral remedies for functional malefic planets and strengthening remedies for weak functional benefic planets through "Kavach" or a "Special Power Kavach" or special purpose Kavach or Gemstones. "Preventive Jyotish Remedies are best."

We all know that the full Moon with the entire starry host and even with all the mountains set on fire cannot fight the darkness of the night. Only the rise of the Sun can bring the night darkness to an end. Similarly, the planetary weaknesses and afflictions can only be reduced to a large extent or even removed with the help of the propitiatory and strengthening astrological remedial measures.

The problems in life are caused by weak planets and/or afflictions to them. To help people overcome their problems, the astrologer advises appropriate astral remedies, such as meditation and spiritual practices, color and gemstone therapy, the wearing of a Kavach or amulet as a protective shield, and the participation in pujas and yagnas, etc. Therefore, a two-way application of astral remedies is administered after diagnosing the problematic planetary influences in a chart. Firstly, the strength is provided to the weak functional benefic planets. The strength can be provided by various methods, e.g. gemstone, color therapy, Kavach (the protective shield containing mystical numbers of the planets) in an auspicious time. Secondly, the malevolence of the functional malefic planets is reduced through the regular practice of meditation, spiritual practices and offering propitiatory charities concerning these planets. The two-way application helps in reducing the impact of functional malefic planetary influences to a large extent. The preventive use of astral remedies is much more useful than the curative astral remedies.

Generally, people seek astral remedies advice in the end after trying all other therapies ignoring the distinct advantage of preventive diagnostic power of the astrological science. It is needless to stress that the benefit of preventive measures as against those of the curative measures is much better.

Whenever performed with faith and sincerity, the efficacy of astral remedies in terms of immediate results depends on many things including the ascendant and the strength of the natal planets. If the functional malefic planets are more in the natal chart, with multiple close afflictions, and the functional benefic planets are weak, one benefits with delay. For example, the people born in the Virgo, Cancer, Pisces, Taurus and Capricorn ascendants need lot of time for sincere and faithful performance of propitiatory remedies. Then the further factors to be seen are the strength of the planets and especially the lord of the operating sub-period and the transit influences.

When to Go for Remedial Measures?

One of the frequently asked questions is what should be the timing of application of astral remedies. Prevention is better than cure. This saying is also true in case of application of astral remedies. No doubt, astral remedies are helpful in a problematic situation but if the native goes for preventive application, it not only proves to be a better tool to tackle various circumstances but also reduces the level of problems to a great extent. The problems are reduced to the level of tension and the potential damage is averted. In many cases we have found that their preventive application has averted dreaded diseases including cancer even when strong combinations for such diseases were present in the horoscope of the person.

To provide strength to the weak birth (natal) planets, we recommend use of gemstone or planetary Kavach as part of Astral or Jyotish remedies for the favorable planets in an auspicious time.

For both - curative and preventive remedies - the judicious mixture of the following astral remedies is applied.

Gems: The ancient wisdom reveals that besides medicines the gemstones and colors are capable of providing good health and mental/spiritual happiness. The efficacy of the gemstones is even recognized by the Ayurveda, the ancient system of medicine.

The importance of time, which means the planetary influences at a particular point of time and at a particular place, has always been recognized since ancient times. The references have been found in the Hindu scriptures, Shakespearean era and the New Testament. It is also firmly believed that the potency of medicines and its curative power increase when the medicine is administered at a particular time of the day and in a particular season. This is also true for the jyotish/astral remedies.

Different planets represent the various colors. To provide strength to the weak natal planets, the divine science of astrology recommends use of gemstone for the favorable planets in an auspicious time. The strength of the planets is raised through the application of influence of concentrated rays of a particular color of a gemstone, which represents a particular planet. The gemstones represent the rays of light peculiar to different planets. The men and women use them for raising the power of planets besides wearing them for ornamental purposes.

Gemstones can be worn in a pendant or in a ring in an auspiciously elected time. Different gemstones are worn in a ring in the following fingers:

Ruby in left ring finger;

Pearl in left little finger;

Red Coral in left/right ring finger;

Emerald in right little finger;

Yellow Sapphire in right index finger;

Diamond in right ring finger;

Blue sapphire in left middle finger.

The gemstones are recommended to begin use in an auspicious time for particular weak planets if they are favorable in one's birth chart. The weight recommended for all the gemstones except diamond is between 4.6 to 4.7 carats. The recommended weight for diamond is 1 carat.

The gemstones for the Sun, the Moon, Mars, Mercury, Jupiter, Venus and Saturn are respectively ruby, pearl, red coral, emerald, yellow sapphire/topaz, diamond or white sapphire/topaz and blue sapphire/topaz, respectively. The gemstone used should be flawless, bright and should not contain feathers and silky inclusions. Only the gemstones pertaining to the functional benefic planets are recommended to be used.

Ruby: This gemstone is used to strengthen the Sun in a horoscope. The Sun represents vitality, the heart as life centre, digestive system and circulatory system of the body, bone structure, constitution, blood, brain, bile, digestive fire, right eye for males and left eye in case of females. It also represents one's father, employment, one's social status and one's relationship with the Government.

If the Sun is weak and/or afflicted in the birth chart, it makes the person vulnerable to sufferings on account of weak eyesight, headaches, erratic blood circulation, heart trouble, bone fractures, overheating, fevers, blood pressure, baldness, neuralgia, bone cancer, etc. If the Sun is a functional benefic planet, the use of ruby protects and promotes the foregoing significations. The recommended weight of the ruby is between 4.6 to 4.7 carats.

Pearl: This gemstone is used to strengthen the Moon in a horoscope. The Moon represents fertility, emotional health and functional health as it governs fluids in body, good quality of blood and lymph, glands, tonsils, breasts, stomach, lymphatic system, face, lungs and chest, and is general significator for sleep and emotional peace. It governs the left eye in the case of males, ovaries, menstrual cycle, uterus, generative organs and right eye in the case of females. It also represents mother, mind and wife.

If the Moon is weak and/or afflicted in the birth chart, besides psychic problems it makes the person vulnerable to sleep disorders, lethargy, drowsiness, auto-immune disorders, lung problems, oral problems (including loss of taste), neurological disorders, epilepsy, digestive complains, water retention, blood disorders, anemia, blood-pressure, enlargement of spleen, diseases of the uterus and ovaries, tuberculosis, menstrual disorders, and the native is vulnerable to frequent cough and cold, fever, lack of appetite, general weakness, etc., and denotes hyper-sensitivity, over-reaction, inability to respond and difficulty in getting in touch with feelings. If the Moon is a functional benefic planet, the use of pearl protects and promotes the foregoing significations. The recommended weight of the pearl is between 4.6 to 4.7 carats.

Red Coral: This gemstone is used to strengthen Mars in a horoscope. Mars represents the chest, bone marrow, blood, bile, digestive fire, intestine, forehead, neck, muscular system, acuity of vision, sinews, nose, external generative organs, physical power and vitality. Mars is also the general significator of younger brothers, which adds to the strength of the native and become a source of strength and courage.

If Mars is weak and/or afflicted in the birth chart, it makes the person vulnerable to inflammations, overheating, inability to tolerate hunger, wounds, burns, accidents, fractures, piles, skin rashes, ulcers, lacerations, operations, all sorts of acute complaints, fevers (particularly eruptive), epilepsy, mental aberration, tumors, cancer in the muscular parts of the body when closely conjunct with Rahu, dysentery, typhoid, cholera, pox and boils, etc., and denotes anger, irritability, haste, impatience, inconstancy, lack of drive and courage, and an 'all-or-nothing' attitude. If Mars is a functional benefic planet, the use of red coral protects and promotes the foregoing significations. The recommended weight of the red coral is between 4.6 to 4.7 carats.

Emerald: This gemstone is of dark green color and bright and is used to strengthen Mercury in a horoscope. Mercury represents the lower part of abdomen, skin, mind, nervous system, urinary bladder, bronchial tube, gastric juice, digestion, intestines, lungs, tongue, mouth, hands and arms. Mercury rules analytical faculties, speech, sharp intellect, power of discrimination and confidence.

If Mercury is weak and/or afflicted in the birth chart, it makes the person vulnerable to psychic diseases, insomnia, nervous breakdown, epilepsy, skin diseases, leucoderma, impotence, loss of memory or speech, vertigo, deafness, asthma, diseases of respiratory canal, auto-immune disorders, disorders of intestines, dyspepsia, etc. It denotes difficulty in thought and communication, timidity, low self-esteem, aloofness, amorality, expediency, over-intellectualization and poor discrimination. Mercury is weak quite frequently. Whenever its period is in operation in any nativity it creates tensions in life, lack of confidence, situation of indecisiveness, etc., which ultimately leads to faulty decisions. The effect is more if Mercury is weak in the birth chart as well as in transit at the time of operation of its sub-periods. It makes a person a nervous wreck and can even cause paralysis when closely afflicted by Rahu-Ketu axis, if the ascendant and its lord are also weak or the sign Virgo falls in the ascendant. If Mercury is a functional benefic planet, the use of emerald protects and promotes the foregoing significations. The recommended weight of the emerald is between 4.6 to 4.7 carats. The gemstone may contain some silky inclusions but it should not contain feathers and black spots.

Yellow Sapphire: This gemstone is recommended to strengthen Jupiter in a horoscope. Jupiter represents the hips, the fat tissue, blood, arterial system, glands, liver, gall bladder, pancreas gland, digestion, absorptive power, ears/hearing power, navel, feet, physical development, palate and throat. Jupiter signifies elder brothers, spouse in female nativities, male progeny, wealth, morals, sincerity, friends, divine grace and father and, in fact, all good things in life.

When weak and/or afflicted, it makes the person vulnerable to lymphatic and circulatory congestion, thrombosis, anemia, tumors, jaundice and other liver complaints, ear problems, dyspepsia, flatulence, cough, cold, diabetes and other diseases of pancreas glands, etc. If Jupiter is a functional benefic planet, the use of yellow sapphire protects and promotes the foregoing significations. The recommended weight of the yellow sapphire is between 4.6 to 4.7 carats.

Diamond: This gemstone is used to strengthen Venus in a horoscope. Venus represents the pelvis and the sexual organs, desires and yearnings, reproduction, the semen/ovum, private parts, kidneys, face, eyes, neck, throat, chin, cheeks, skin, venous system, etc. Venus is also the general significator of wife.

When weak and/or afflicted, it makes the person vulnerable to venereal diseases, diseases of urinary or reproductive system, diabetes, stones in bladder or kidneys, cataract, weakness of sexual organs, cough, cold, sexual perversions, impotence or inability to have sexual relations, loss of body luster, etc. If Venus is a functional benefic planet, the use of diamond protects and promotes the foregoing significations. The recommended weight of the diamond is one carat. The gemstone should be flawless and should not contain silky inclusions.

Blue Sapphire: This gemstone is of dark blue color and is used to strengthen Saturn in a horoscope. Saturn represents the nerve tissue, tendons, joints, spleen, teeth, knees, shin and part of leg between ankle and knee, gall bladder, phlegm and secretive system, respiratory system and bones.

When weak and/or afflicted, it makes the person vulnerable to constant and painful diseases, all sorts of chronic and degenerative diseases, leg fracture, cancer, diseases of glands, paralysis, arthritis, rheumatism, gout, rickets, consumption, flatulence, deformities, coldness of the body, nerve disorders, insanity, numbness, windy diseases, senility, impotence in men, pain and obstruction in the functions of the body like retention of urine, intestinal obstruction, etc. If Saturn is a functional benefic planet, the use of blue sapphire protects and promotes the foregoing significations. The recommended weight of the blue sapphire is between 4.6 to 4.7 carats. The gemstone should be flawless and should not contain feathers and silky inclusions.

Kavach

The design and concept of Kavach in this book, has been created, tested and popularized by Author and Astrologer Shri V. K. Choudhry.

Kavach Design Copyright (C) 1994 Shri V. K. Choudhry.

Kavach is in the form of a silver/white metal pendant. For some ascending signs the size of Kavach is 4.5 cm x 2 cm approximately while for other ascending signs the size of the Kavach is 3 cm x 2 cm approximately. Kavach can also be created in special designs and in gold.

Kavach also called an amulet or a zodiac pendant is a protective shield in the form of a pendant which is made of silver containing mystical numbers of the functional benefic planets in a nativity and is a strengthening measure, providing protection to the natal and transit afflictions of the weak functional benefic planets. Kavach is energized in an auspiciously elected time. With its use, the weak planets are enabled to protect and promote their significations. The Kavach draws its power from the powerful planetary position in which it is created and it is worn also in a specially elected auspicious time for generating the desired impact. Kavach carries the spiritual blessings of the provider of the Kavach and is used for improving the strength of the planets to enable them to bear the natal and transit afflictions.

Kavach is certainly not a miraculous or magical object. This is part of faith healing and its effectiveness and the amount of help cannot be measured in a scientific manner. The confidence of the Kavach providers is based on the feedback of the users. This is used both for preventive and curative purposes, and dispenses with the necessity of wearing different gems for different planets.

Effectiveness of Kavach

Effectiveness of Kavach and other astral remedies depends on many things including the ascendant and the strength of the natal planets. If the functional malefic planets are more in the natal chart with multiple close afflictions and the functional benefic planets are weak, the person benefits with delay. For example, the people born in the Virgo, Cancer, Pisces, Taurus and Capricorn ascendants after wearing the Kavach need lot of time with simultaneous, sincere and faithful performance of propitiatory remedies to get the benefits of the Kavach. Then the further factors to be seen are the strength of the planets, especially of the lord of the operating sub-period, and the transit influences.

Those having the exact afflictions of the most malefic planet or the functional malefic planets amongst themselves or with the functional benefic planets may not appreciate immediately the impact made by the Kavach or a special power Kavach. Such persons need a special purpose Kavach which consists of special power Kavach and the gemstones. But in fact, the Kavach or special power Kavach is believed to provide tremendous support to the planets under stress. For example, the exact affliction in the case of the lords of the sixth and eighth houses makes one vulnerable to paralytic attacks or chronic ailments. The application of an appropriate Kavach here is believed to reduce the vulnerability to a large extent but how much is difficult to show. Such exact afflictions are very difficult to remove.

Power of Kavach:

To generate good healing power, the Kavach provider astrologer should have any one of the following planetary influence in his/her birth chart:

i)   a strong or at least well-placed and unafflicted Jupiter in his/her own natal chart.

ii) a strong fourth or first lord in the ninth house or a strong lord of the ninth house in the fourth or second or first house with an unafflicted Sun.

The Kavach gets power to do well not only due to the engravings being done in an auspicious time but also due to a prescribed way of life followed by the Kavach provider. The astrologer prescribing and providing use of the Kavach should follow these principles:

- Bath in the morning without any bed tea, etc.

- Prayers to Lord.

- Performance of propitiatory remedies as per one's own chart.

- Practice the divine way in life i.e. (1) Be content; (2) Increase utility to humanity; (3) Help poor and needy; (4) Be kind, generous and benevolent; and (5) Avoid deeper involvement in sensual pleasures, anger, pride, greed and envy.

Continuous practice of the above principles helps in generating spiritual power for helping others to ward off evils in life and derive benefits indicated by the functional benefic planets in one's chart.

Kavach Information

Kavach is worn in auspiciously elected time. The auspicious time is worked out with reference to the place of stay. Gemstone therapy has limited utility in comparison to the benefits gained by wearing the Kavach. The Kavach acts as a protective shield and at a cost which is far less than the cost of wearing four to six precious gemstones. So, make your life better by strengthening weak birth planets with a Kavach. When used as a preventive therapy it is likely to help in the following matters:-

- Energizes weak birth planets for bringing happiness in life

- Success in studies

- Success in professional career/business

- Develops leadership skills

- Improves memory and analytical skills

- Protects health

- Gives timely marriage

- Gives success in relationships

- Blesses with children

-       Blesses with achievements and recognition in life and so on
        and so forth the list is very long.

        The details required for providing a "Kavach" are:

1.   Horoscope details - that is date, time and place of birth of the
        person who desires to have a Kavach.

2.   The details of place of stay in the next couple of months for
        the person to wear the Kavach with longitudes, latitudes and
        summer time correction, if any.

3.   The complete postal address for dispatch of Kavach through
        registered post (air-mail).

        The Kavach can be worn in a thread or a gold/silver chain
around the neck and after one starts wearing the Kavach for the
first time one should continuously wear it. There is no precaution
to be taken by the wearer of the Kavach.

        Those who are metal sensitive or have strong aesthetic sense
can derive benefits of Kavach by carrying it with them in their
wallet or keeping it at the place of worship in the home.

        If it is mandatory to take the Kavach off the body, one can do
that but should again wear the Kavach as soon as it is possible to
derive the impact of the Kavach continuously. The thread of the
Kavach can be changed, whenever it requires a change.

        The details of mystical numbers for all the twelve ascendants
which can be engraved on both sides of the Kavach or Amulet or
Zodiac Pendant are being given in the following pages.

ARIES ASCENDANT

Mystical Numbers **Mystical Numbers**

DESIGN

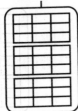

6	1	8
7	5	3
2	9	4

7	2	9
8	6	4
3	10	5

8	3	10
9	7	5
4	11	6

10	5	12
11	9	7
6	13	8

11	6	13
12	10	8
7	14	9

12	7	14
13	11	9
8	15	10

TAURUS ASCENDANT

Mystical Numbers **Mystical Numbers**

DESIGN

7	2	9
8	6	4
3	10	5

6	1	8
7	5	3
2	9	4

9	4	11
10	8	6
5	12	7

12	7	14
13	11	9
8	15	10

GEMINI ASCENDANT

Mystical Numbers **Mystical Numbers**

DESIGN

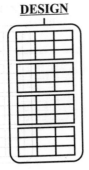

10	5	12
11	9	7
6	13	8

7	2	9
8	6	4
3	10	5

6	1	8
7	5	3
2	9	4

11	6	13
12	10	8
7	14	9

9	4	11
10	8	6
5	12	7

8	3	10
9	7	5
4	11	6

12	7	14
13	11	9
8	15	10

CANCER ASCENDANT

DESIGN

Mystical
Numbers

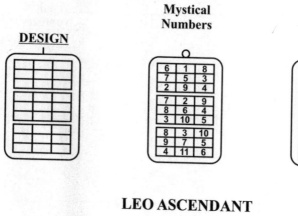

Mystical
Numbers

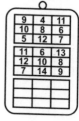

LEO ASCENDANT

DESIGN

Mystical
Numbers

Mystical
Numbers

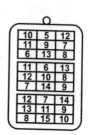

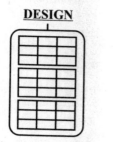

VIRGO ASCENDANT

DESIGN

Mystical
Numbers

Mystical
Numbers

LIBRA ASCENDANT

DESIGN

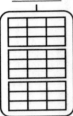

Mystical Numbers

6	1	8
7	5	3
2	9	4

7	2	9
8	6	4
3	10	5

8	3	10
9	7	5
4	11	6

Mystical Numbers

10	5	12
11	9	7
6	13	8

11	6	13
12	10	8
7	14	9

12	7	14
13	11	9
8	15	10

SCORPIO ASCENDANT

DESIGN

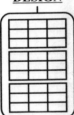

Mystical Numbers

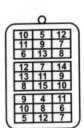

10	5	12
11	9	7
6	13	8

12	7	14
13	11	9
8	15	10

9	4	11
10	8	6
5	12	7

Mystical Numbers

6	1	8
7	5	3
2	9	4

7	2	9
8	6	4
3	10	5

SAGITTARIUS ASCENDANT

DESIGN

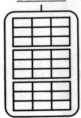

Mystical Numbers

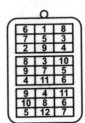

6	1	8
7	5	3
2	9	4

8	3	10
9	7	5
4	11	6

9	4	11
10	8	6
5	12	7

Mystical Numbers

10	5	12
11	9	7
6	13	8

11	6	13
12	10	8
7	14	9

12	7	14
13	11	9
8	15	10

CAPRICORN ASCENDANT

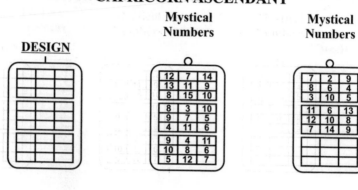

DESIGN

Mystical Numbers

12	7	14
13	11	9
8	15	10

8	3	10
9	7	5
4	11	6

9	4	11
10	8	6
5	12	7

Mystical Numbers

7	2	9
8	6	4
3	10	5

11	6	13
12	10	8
7	14	9

AQUARIUS ASCENDANT

DESIGN

Mystical Numbers

12	7	14
13	11	9
8	15	10

8	3	10
9	7	5
4	11	6

11	6	13
12	10	8
7	14	9

Mystical Numbers

6	1	8
7	5	3
2	9	4

10	5	12
11	9	7
6	13	8

PISCES ASCENDANT

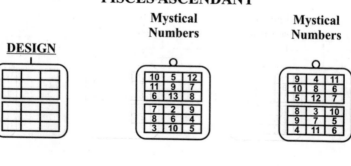

DESIGN

Mystical Numbers

10	5	12
11	9	7
6	13	8

7	2	9
8	6	4
3	10	5

Mystical Numbers

9	4	11
10	8	6
5	12	7

8	3	10
9	7	5
4	11	6

Color Therapy: This is a very potent preventive remedy for epilepsy, mental retardation, psychic problems, etc. and is practiced through the use of favorable colors in the matters of dress and furnishings in one's living room. As each day of the week is ruled by a particular planet, each day we should dress at least one wearable garment of the color indicated for that planet if functional benefic.

These are the days of the week and the colors ruled by each planet:

Sun	Sunday	Orange, Pink, Golden
Moon	Monday	White, Silver
Mars	Tuesday	Burning Red
Mercury	Wednesday	Dark Green
Jupiter	Thursday	Yellow
Venus	Friday	Variegated, Royal Blue
Saturn	Saturday	Black, Dark Brown, Navy Blue

As per the opinion of experts compiled by a Library in Pittsburgh, the grey color of cars was found to be the worst in car safety. As per our color therapy, we had always been suggesting to avoid grey colors by those desirous of happy living and good health.

Vastu: Again this is a preventive as well as a curative therapy for solving the problems in physical and spiritual areas. Wider applications of this therapy are in the field of success of professional ventures. This is practiced through the use of proper outlay of a building to derive geo-magnetic forces for properly energizing the total impact of that building with the help of light, air, space and aura conducive to the main function of the environment.

The minimum vastu to be kept in view is:

1. Place of meditation in north east;

2. Bedrooms in south and south west;

3. Children's study in north;

4. Kitchen in south east;

5. Stairs in south-west;

6. Heavy structures in the house in south-west;

7. One should sleep with one's head in east, or south or south west directions;

8. The central place of the residential unit should be empty;

9. There should be openings in east and west and it would be better if the opening is also in south direction;

10. The opening only in south direction creates conflicts and diseases while the openings only in north direction stops family prosperity and sometimes even continuity. Opening only in the west direction brings poverty.

11. The place should be properly lit and pastel colors of functional benefic planets should be used on the walls;

12. The furnishings should be mostly plain or with very little flowery designs. In any case the patterns and designs on the fabric should not be too imposing.

Mantras: As part of the meditation, the recitation of Mantras is prescribed for propitiating the trouble causing planets.

Charities: These are offered for the functional malefic planets causing afflictions/problems in a horoscope. The malefic influences are effectively tackled with the help of one of these propitiatory remedial measures for each planet when acting as a functional malefic:

Sun:

• Serving one's father or helping old age needy persons.

• Give wheat soaked in water with 20 grams of jaggery (Gur) to a cow on Sundays.

• Surya Namaskar at sunrise.

* Observe law of the land meticulously.

Moon:

* Serving one's mother or old age women.
* Keep a fresh water pot for the birds.
* Offering boiled rice with sugar to the birds.

Mars:

* Service or help to younger brother(s).
* Prayers/meditation every morning for at least 10 min.
* Being considerate to one's servant(s).
* Exercising patience.

Mercury:

* Helping poor students and needy children.
* Donating to orphanages, twice a year.
* Offering green fodder (about 2 Kg) to a cow.
* Donating green pulses.

Jupiter:

* Offering service to one's preceptor/teacher.
* Prayers/meditation every morning.
* Offering banana in small pieces to the birds.
* Offering one bundi laddu (an Indian sweet of yellow color) or any yellow sweet to the birds.

Venus:

* Being considerate to one's wife or helping ladies in distress.
* Donating sugar, rice and cooking oil.

- Offering white sweets to the birds.
- Donating silken clothes of bright colors.

Saturn:

- Being considerate to servants.
- Offering simple salty food to the birds.
- Donating black pulses or salt or mustard oil on Saturdays.
- Donate to organizations that help poor people, twice a year.

Rahu:

- Serving one's parents.
- Give part of your breakfast to the birds.
- Donate for old age needy persons or lepers, twice a year.
- Giving away brown colored sweets to the birds.

Ketu:

- Offering some food to a street dog.
- Donate for the old age homes, twice a year.
- Prayers to Lord Ganapathi.
- Serving/helping institutions or persons working for spiritualism.

These remedies are to be performed daily in the morning after bath but before breakfast. In case the native is unable to do so as in the case of sickness or if he/she is out of town or in the case of children, these remedial measures can be performed by parents or spouse. If the offering is not accepted by a dog or cow, another dog/cow should be tried. The remedial measures should be performed regularly and the performance of any one of the suggested measures for a particular planet would suffice.

The weakness of the significator planets, as indicated earlier, is made up with the help of a specially prepared Kavach to be worn by the native in an auspiciously elected time.

Ascendant-wise Tested Household Jyotish/ Astral Remedies/Propitiatory Measures for Afflicting Planets.

Aries Ascendant

1. Offering a sweet parantha (Indian pancake stuffed with sugar and fried) in small pieces to crows daily in the morning for Rahu.

2. Offering breakfast/lunch to lepers on Fridays for Rahu.

3. Offering some slices of bread dipped in milk to street dogs daily in the morning after morning prayers for Ketu.

4. Offering green fodder/vegetables for cows daily for Mercury.

Taurus Ascendant

1. Offering a sweet parantha (Indian pancake stuffed with sugar and fried) in small pieces to crows daily in the morning for Rahu.

2. Offering breakfast/lunch to lepers on Fridays for Rahu.

3. Offering some slices of bread dipped in milk to street dogs daily in the morning for Ketu.

4. Offering morning prayers daily and prasad in temple on Tuesdays for Mars.

5. Offering Bundi Laddus/yellow colored sweet to crows daily in the morning for Jupiter.

6. Offering white colored sweets like Rasgulla or kheer to crows daily in the morning for Venus.

Gemini Ascendant

1.   Offering a sweet parantha (Indian pancake stuffed with sugar and fried) in small pieces to crows daily in the morning for Rahu.

2.   Offering breakfast/lunch to lepers on Fridays for Rahu.

3.   Offering some slices of bread dipped in milk to street dogs daily in the morning after morning prayers for Ketu.

Cancer Ascendant

1.   Offering a sweet parantha (Indian pancake stuffed with sugar and fried) in small pieces to crows daily in the morning for Rahu.

2.   Offering breakfast/lunch to lepers on Fridays for Rahu.

3.   Offering some slices of bread dipped in milk to street dogs daily in the morning after morning prayers for Ketu.

4.   Offering Bundi Laddus/yellow colored sweet to crows daily in the morning for Jupiter.

5.   Offering home made Indian bread (roti) with salt and mustard oil in small pieces to crows daily in the morning for Saturn.

Leo Ascendant

1.   Offering a sweet parantha (Indian pancake stuffed with sugar and fried) in small pieces to crows daily in the morning for Rahu.

2.   Offering breakfast/lunch to lepers on Fridays for Rahu.

3.   Offering some slices of bread dipped in milk to street dogs daily in the morning after morning prayers for Ketu.

4.   Keeping a fresh pot of water for the birds daily in the morning for the Moon.

Virgo Ascendant

1. Offering a sweet parantha (Indian pancake stuffed with sugar and fried) in small pieces to crows daily in the morning for Rahu.

2. Offering breakfast/lunch to lepers on Fridays for Rahu.

3. Offering some slices of bread dipped in milk to street dogs daily in the morning after morning prayers for Ketu.

4. Offering morning prayers daily and prasad in temple on Tuesdays for Mars.

5. Offering sweet food made of wheat, jaggery and in milk to a cow for the Sun daily in the morning or on Sundays depending upon the level of affliction in the chart.

6. Offering roti (home made bread) with salt and mustard oil in small pieces to crows daily in the morning for Saturn.

Libra Ascendant

1. Offering a sweet parantha (Indian pancake stuffed with sugar and fried) in small pieces to crows daily in the morning for Rahu.

2. Offering breakfast/lunch to lepers on Fridays for Rahu.

3. Offering some slices of bread dipped in milk to street dogs daily in the morning after morning prayers for Ketu.

4. Offering green fodder/vegetables for cows daily for Mercury.

Scorpio Ascendant

1. Offering a sweet parantha (Indian pancake stuffed with sugar and fried) in small pieces to crows daily in the morning for Rahu.

2. Offering breakfast/lunch to lepers on Fridays for Rahu.

3. Offering some slices of bread dipped in milk to street dogs daily in the morning after morning prayers for Ketu.

4.   Offering morning prayers daily and prasad in temple on Tuesdays for Mars.

5.   Offering white colored sweets like Rasgulla or Kheer to crows daily in the morning for Venus.

Sagittarius Ascendant

1.   Offering a sweet parantha (Indian pancake stuffed with sugar and fried) in small pieces to crows daily in the morning for Rahu.

2.   Offering breakfast/lunch to lepers on Fridays for Rahu.

3.   Offering some slices of bread dipped in milk to street dogs daily in the morning after morning prayers for Ketu.

4.   Keeping a fresh pot of water for the birds daily in the morning for the Moon.

Capricorn Ascendant

1.   Offering a sweet parantha (Indian pancake stuffed with sugar and fried) in small pieces to crows daily in the morning for Rahu.

2.   Offering breakfast/lunch to lepers on Fridays for Rahu.

3.   Offering some slices of bread dipped in milk to street dogs daily in the morning after morning prayers for Ketu.

4.   Offering Bundi Laddus/yellow colored sweet to crows daily in the morning for Jupiter.

5.   Offering sweet food made of wheat, jaggery and in milk to a cow for the Sun daily in the morning or on Sundays depending upon the level of affliction in the chart.

Aquarius Ascendant

1.   Offering a sweet parantha (Indian pancake stuffed with sugar and fried) in small pieces to crows daily in the morning for Rahu.

2.   Offering breakfast/lunch to lepers on Fridays for Rahu.

3.   Offering some slices of bread dipped in milk to street dogs daily in the morning after morning prayers for Ketu.

4.   Keeping a fresh pot of water for the birds daily in the morning for the Moon.

5.   Offering green fodder/vegetables for cows daily for Mercury.

Pisces Ascendant

1.   Offering a sweet parantha (Indian pancake stuffed with sugar and fried) in small pieces to crows daily in the morning for Rahu.

2.   Offering breakfast/lunch to lepers on Fridays for Rahu.

3.   Offering some slices of bread dipped in milk to street dogs daily in the morning after morning prayers for Ketu.

4.   Offering roti (home made bread) with salt and mustard oil in small pieces to crows daily in the morning for Saturn.

5.   Offering sweet food made of wheat, jaggery and in milk to a cow for the Sun daily in the morning or on Sundays depending upon the level of affliction in the chart.

6.   Offering white colored sweets like Rasgulla or kheer to crows daily in the morning for Venus.

Notes:

1.   **Bundi Laddu is an Indian sweet of yellow color.**

2.   **Rasgulla is an Indian sweet of white color.**

3.   **Kheer is rice cooked in milk and sugar is added.**

4.   **In place of a sweet parantha a piece of brown cake can be given.**

Chapter 3

Indications of Planets
in Malefic Houses

People seek help from the divine science of astrology when they are in suspense, persisting distress and are facing uncertainties and anxiety in life. They want to know about the duration and the result of the uncertainty. They also seek advice to redress their concern, as well. Help seekers are from all walks of life, crossing the bars of caste, creed and religion. The divine science of reading planetary influences was used all over the world in one form or the other. It is not concerned with any religion. As the Sun gives light and energy to one and all across the world so is its influence based on its position in the horoscope drawn for a person for the time of his/her birth.

A man is troubled by ill health, insolvency, disputes, accidents, obstructions, hospitalization, punishment by the state, enmity, etc. We all know that these aspects are governed by the malefic houses of a birth chart. The houses are the sixth, eighth and the twelfth houses. The results pertaining to these houses are felt (i) during the sub-periods of the planets placed in these houses depending upon their respective strength and (ii) the lords of these houses causing close afflictions in the chart. Based on this simple technique the divine science can foretell the incidence of the difficult times and the areas of difficulties. It can also suggest ways and means to reduce the impact of the difficulties to a large extent. The wisest creation of the God, the man, learnt to augment the potentialities in the chart. A happy and content man is an asset for the society as he can help people in distress during the spare time available with him.

All planets placed in malefic houses show trouble. The trouble is to the significations ruled by these badly planets. The troubles come in their operating sub-periods and during the course of transit afflictions by malefic planets.

The functional malefic lords indicate trouble when they cause exact or close afflictions in the birth chart. The trouble pertains to the significations of the houses or the planets under the close affliction of the lords of the malefic houses.

The functional malefic lords give results concerning the positive aspects of the houses ruled by them as per their strength. When weak they give the results of lower order. When the functional malefic lords themselves are weak and afflicted, the significations ruled by them are lost.

The two key areas for the analysis of the horoscopes are the functional nature of the planets in a particular nativity and the relationships developed by the planets with other planets and houses. The relationship is developed through conjunction or aspects by planets with other planets or the most effective points of the houses and their placements in various houses. While the placement of a planet affects the significations ruled by it, its impact on the house of its placement would be only applicable if it forms close conjunction/aspect with its most effective point. Any planet posited within 5 degrees (on either side) of the most effective point of any house would be making its impact on the said house, depending of course upon the strength and functional nature of the planet under consideration. This planet also fully influences the house(s) aspected by it.

Malefic planet is considered strong when it is not weak. Malefic planet is considered weak due to infancy, old age, combustion, bad placement in houses other than its own, debilitation, affliction, placement in an afflicted house, debilitation in navamsa and due to weakness/affliction of its dispositor.

The positive traits of malefic houses, which contain mooltrikona sign(s), fructify when their lords are strong, or well placed and unafflicted.

The positive traits of the malefic houses are as under :-

The Sixth House: Sound financial position, victory over enemies and no apprehension of losses through disputes, cheating, theft and fire.

The Eighth house: Long life, financial gains to the father, gains through inheritance, gains through draw of lots and unearned wealth, continuity of marital tie, etc.

The Twelfth house: Good sleep, staying together with the spouse, gains from foreign lands, no apprehension of imprisonment and hospitalizations, comforts and luxurious life.

Let us see a current example showing how the placement of twelfth lord in the eighth house in the country chart of Ukraine unleashed anarchy involving loss of life, peace and property for the country during the sub period of a badly placed twelfth lord. The 2014 Ukrainian revolution began on November 21, 2013, with a series of violent episodes of civil unrest in the Euromaiden protests against the government for turning away from closer integration with the European Union to the west in favour of forging closer ties with Russia to the east. The conflict escalated rapidly, leading to the downfall of the government on February 21, 2014, with President Yanukovich fleeing the capital. A new government was set up within a few days. President Yanukovich re-surfaced in Russia where he gave a press conference stating that he was still the elected President of Ukraine. On February 27-28, Russian military forces invaded the Crimea region of Ukraine, effectively taking control of it. The well placed Saturn, Moon and Mars as also the lord of the eighth in the eighth house show that the country is likely to stay on the world map. The closely afflicted Venus and Mercury show that there will be foreign intervention of neighbours in solving their problems. In the process due to exact affliction of Jupiter to the eighth, second and fourth houses shows that the country will incur a loss of some of its resources including land. The transgression of the territorial integrity of a country by neighbouring or other counties is analysed through the strength of the lord of the tenth house and the involvement of the twelfth lord in influencing the ascendant, second, fourth, eighth and tenth houses. In this case the tenth lord is weak, badly placed and under close affliction of the functional malefic planets, Jupiter and the Sun. And Jupiter as a twelfth lord influences eighth, second and fourth houses.

Example Chart 7

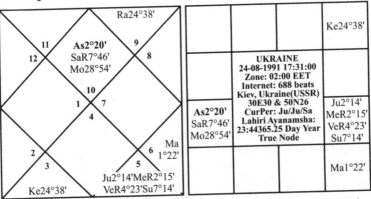

During the sub period of Jupiter with transit Jupiter in the sixth house, it happened to be conflict and controversial time involving losses for the Ukraine nation. Added to this was the prolonged transit impact of Rahu-Ketu axis in the Ukraine chart on the ascending degree and the badly placed planets in the eighth house - Jupiter, Mercury, Venus and the Sun.

This is the result of twelfth lord in the eighth house in the country chart. The results are shown in the sub period of Jupiter being twelfth lord in its own main period. At the time of this event Jupiter was traveling in the sixth house of conflicts and injuries. This is in line with reading sub period results techniques contained in this book.

The subject will be discussed further with the help of case studies.

Chart 1

Female born 14th May 1967, 1725 Hrs. Jalandhar, India.

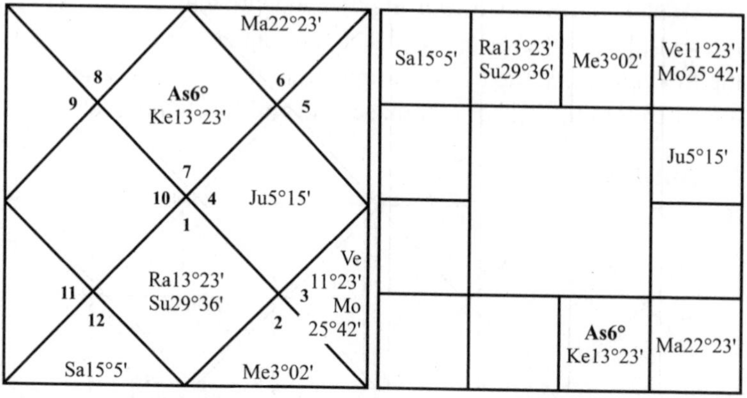
Ma22°23'
8
9
As6°
Ke13°23'
6
5
7
10
4
Ju5°15'
1
Ve
11°23'
11
Ra13°23'
Su29°36'
3
Mo
12
2
25°42'
Sa15°5'
Me3°02'
Sa15°5'
Ra13°23'
Su29°36'
Me3°02'
Ve11°23'
Mo25°42'
Ju5°15'
As6°
Ke13°23'
Ma22°23'

Three planets are placed in malefic houses. These are Saturn, Mars and Mercury. The significations ruled by these badly placed planets are rendered weak. The functional malefic planet, Mercury, closely afflicts the most effective point of the eighth house. Venus rules health in general and longevity. Besides other things, the Saturn rules the progeny matters, stomach and emotions. Mars is significator for health in general and rules the health of the spouse. Mercury rules comforts. The eighth house rules longevity and inheritance. The second house rules wealth, continuance of family line and status. The Sun, significator of vitality and stomach, is very weak in the nativity due to extreme old age. The native was not blessed with a child, she had bad health and during the sub-period of Mercury in its own main period the native was diagnosed for a tumor in stomach in advanced stage, endangering her life. In such severe afflictions while the preventive astral remedies could have been of a great help, the curative astral remedies are not of much help.

Chart 2

Male born 23rd December 1954, 2115 Hrs., New Delhi, India.

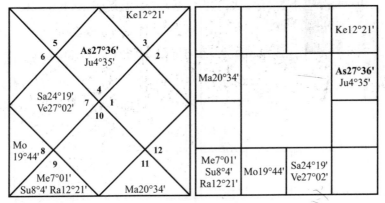

Jupiter and Saturn rule malefic houses due to their mooltrikona signs in the sixth and eighth houses, respectively. The Sun, Mercury, Rahu, Mars and Ketu are placed in malefic houses. Jupiter ruling the house of disputes is in the ascendant and the lord of the eighth house, Saturn, ruling obstructions and death, closely afflicts the lord of the fourth house and the most effective point of the fourth house. The fourth house rules education and mother besides domestic happiness in particular. The lord of the second house, the Sun, ruling wealth and family is badly placed in the house of disputes. The Sun is also closely conjunct with Rahu and afflicted. The main significations in the chart are disputes connected with family, marriage and assets and threatened loss of these. The native faced obstructions in education, has simple graduation and his mother suffered widowhood early in life. During the main period of the Sun, the wife deserted the native and there was a dispute regarding the assets.

Chart 3

Male born 11th November 1980, 1930 Hrs., Gurgaon, India.

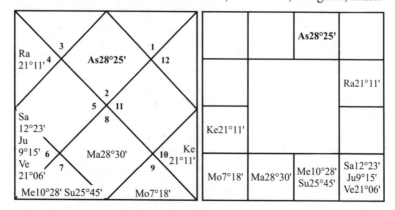

The planets ruling the third, fourth and fifth houses are badly placed in malefic houses. The functional malefic Jupiter is closely conjunct with the lord of the tenth house, Saturn. The functional malefic Mars closely afflicts the seventh, tenth, first and second houses. The well placed but debilitated functional malefic Venus is under the close affliction of Ketu. The weakness and the bad placement of the fourth lord caused numerous difficulties to mother including a divorce within four years of marriage besides spoiling the school education of the child. Lack of good education resulted in difficulties in the area of earning livelihood, which is indicated by the afflicted lord of the tenth house. The well placed Jupiter, though weak due to weakness of the dispositor, blessed the native with inheritance in the form of a dwelling unit owned by the mother. The astral remedies were sought when the performance of native was very poor in her middle school. Wearing of a Kavach and performance of propitiatory remedies for the afflicting functional malefic planets resulted in graduation studies though not with good marks. The native is continuing his studies with his job.

Chart 4

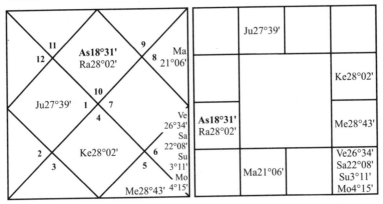

Mercury, ruling the ninth house, is placed in the eighth house. The functional malefic Jupiter is in the fourth house and is closely afflicting Mercury placed in a malefic house. The other functional malefic, the Sun, is placed in the ninth house and is closely conjunct with the lord of the seventh house. Apart from this, there is a close conjunction (within a longitudinal difference of 5 degrees) of Saturn with Venus and the most effective point of the ninth house. During the sub-period of Jupiter in the main period of Jupiter, the parents of the native and the domestic peace received a great setback. During the sub-period of Saturn, the improvements eluded as the severe affliction of the ninth lord did not allow the well placed and functional benefic Saturn to bestow good results. During the sub-period of Mercury in the main period of Jupiter, the fortune of the native saw many reversals through losses to husband, financial crisis to self and parents, etc. The astral remedies have been able to put a stop to further misfortunes and has developed some good results but find it difficult to make the native happy.

Chart 5

Female born 15th October 1974, 1024 Hrs. 76E01 30N22 India.

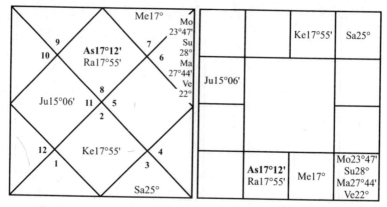

Saturn, ruling the fourth house and Mercury, ruling the eleventh house, are placed in malefic houses. Mars and Venus, being functional malefic planets, cause severe afflictions to the Moon and the Sun besides afflicting each other. The fourth, ninth, twelfth, eleventh and the tenth houses are involved besides affliction of the Sun and the Moon ruling parents, general fortune, profession and the heart. Rahu-Ketu axis is conjunct with the most effective points of the houses of its location and afflicts all the houses occupied and aspected. The overall impact of the planetary position resulted in lack of elder brother, difficulties to parents, obstruction in education caused by severe health problems of hypertension and fits at a very young age of sixteen years. The father of the native suffered with prolonged illness due to paralysis. The planetary position is indicative of problematic finances and profession. The application of curative astral remedies in the form of wearing a Kavach for strengthening the weak functional benefic planets, charities for the functional malefic planets - Mars, Venus, Rahu and Ketu - and use of dress strictly as per the suitable colors, were able to reduce the incidence of fits and hypertension to a large extent. The astral remedies enabled the native to pursue her studies more vigorously.

Chart 6

Male born 23rd January 1971, 0720 Hrs. New Delhi, India.

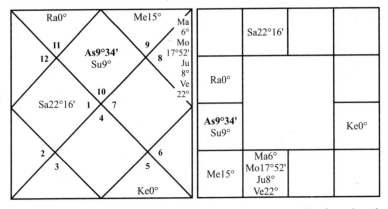

Ketu and Mercury are placed in malefic houses. The functional malefic Jupiter forms a close conjunction/aspect with the most effective point of the eleventh house and afflicts the houses occupied and aspected. The other functional malefic planet, the Sun, is conjunct with the most effective point of the ascendant and afflicts both the ascendant and the seventh house. The Sun also becomes weak due to placement in an afflicted house. The planets placed in the eleventh house become weak due to the close affliction to the MEP of the said house. The weak Mars gets closely afflicted. The conjunction of the eighth lord with the ascendant gave a severe accident. The close affliction to the lord of the fourth house and the debilitation of the Moon – the significator for mother - gave early widowhood to the mother besides playing havoc with the married life of the native. Before application of the astral remedies in the form of a Kavach and propitiatory remedial measures for the functional malefic planets, the Sun, Jupiter, Rahu and Ketu, the planetary influences in this case resulted in early loss of father and a severe accident involving multiple fractures keeping the native in bed for over six months. However, the native found improvements with the astral remedies and has been able to ward off the evils in the matters of happiness in marriage.

Chart 7

Indian Independence Chart, 15th August 1947, 0000 Hrs. New Delhi, India.

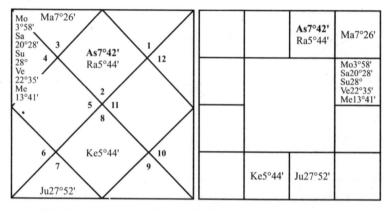

The functional malefic lord of the eighth house is placed in the sixth house connecting death with inimical relations, diseases and financial difficulties. The country faced four wars, proxy war with terrorism and a number of natural calamities involving mass deaths. The functional malefic lord of the twelfth house is placed on the most effective point of the second house ruling status, harmonious relationship amongst various sections of the society and wealth. During the sub-period of the functional malefic Mars, the country lost its status in the eyes of world due to large number of financial scams and scandals like, hawala, fodder scam, broad gauge conversion, political bribery to MPs, allotment of houses and agencies, etc. besides the continuous unfavorable foreign trade and rising foreign and internal debt. The functional malefic Venus closely afflicts Saturn resulting into various political parties fighting to gain ruling power in the country. The placement of exalted Rahu close with the most effective point of the ascendant explains the loss of moral character by many, incidence of various scams and generation of black money. The transit malefic influence of Rahu/ Ketu on the natal Rahu, Ketu and the Moon in end of March, 1997, resulted into a political chaos in the country due to withdrawal of support by a political party to the ruling front. In January 2001 the state of Gujarat suffered from a massive earthquake resulting into great loss of life. In last week of December, 2004, the southern states of India were assaulted by the Tsunami in which thousands lost lives.

Chart 8

Male born 8th February 1959, 0701 Hrs. 77E40 28N36, India.

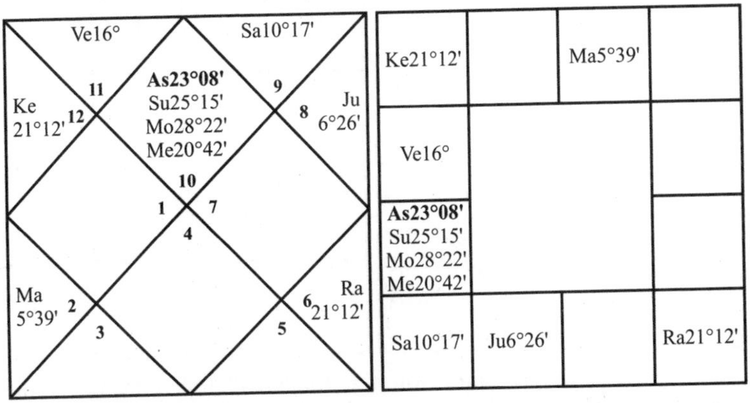

See the impact of the functional malefic lords in this nativity. The Sun afflicts the most effective point of the ascendant, the most effective point of seventh house and the Moon and Mercury. Jupiter afflicts the lord of the fourth house. The lord of the second house is placed in the twelfth house, which is a malefic house. The bad placement of the lord of the second house and severe affliction to weak Mars and the lords of the seventh and ninth houses resulted into the early loss of parental happiness, lack of good school education and denied material possessions in life. The main period of Rahu operating from the ninth house gave involvement in the religious organization. Due to the bad health on account of heart trouble and hypertension in early stages of life, the native decided to remain unmarried and to go in for the life of a religious preacher. Jupiter is strongly placed in the birth chart and influences the planet ruling inclinations. The weak lord of the second house and the afflicted lords of the fourth and seventh houses and the severe affliction of the most malefic planet to the most effective point of the seventh house clearly indicate the lack of happiness from marital/family life. The native wears a Kavach to safeguard his deteriorating health.

Chart 9

Male born in March 1946.

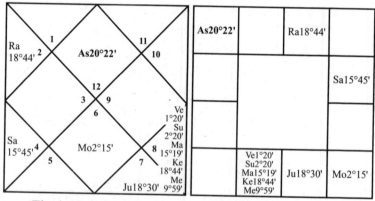

The lord of the tenth house is placed in the malefic eighth house but its close impact on the most effective point of the second house is indicative of acquiring status in life through self-effort. The functional malefic Saturn is well placed but suffers from the close aspect of Ketu. The functional malefic Sun closely afflicts the functional malefic Venus, in the ninth house. The well placed lord of the second house also suffers from the close conjunction of Ketu. During the main period of the badly placed lord of the tenth house and in the sub-period of the functional malefic Sun, the native was involved in a career reversal and was involved in a scandalous investigation in one of the scams of the country. The placement of Rahu in its sign of exaltation, near the most effective point of the third house made the native ambitious for rise in life. The lord of the house of easy gains is closely conjunct with the royal planet, the Sun. But the weakness of both the Sun and Venus lack retention or protection power.

Chapter 4

Timing of Events

Timing Recovery of Patients

Diverse applications of astrology include timing of events. Timing of events is done with the help of the sub-periods and the triple transit triggering influence of planets in the natal chart. Let us take up the study of timing recovery and survival of patients. In an atmosphere of suspense when medical attendants can't assure or clearly spell out the condition of the patient to the querent (person asking question) about the condition of the patient or the prolonged treatment is not bringing improvement, one is impelled to turn to astrology to know the likely end of the suspense and the timing. The serious illness is governed by the following factors:-

i) The sub-periods of weak and afflicted natal planets.

ii) The sub-period of the planet whose mooltrikona sign falls in the sixth house whenever such a sixth lord forms a close conjunction/aspect with another natal/transit planet or most effective point of a particular house.

iii) The illness is triggered by the triple transit malefic influence on the weak natal/transit planetary configurations. Sometimes the prolonged transit influence may run from three months to eight or nine months. For example the close impact of Saturn at 25 degrees in 2014 prevails for about nine months. For those persons who are born in the ascending signs of Cancer, Virgo and Pisces at or around 25 degrees the whole year of 2014 will be quite difficult. If these persons have some planet at or around 25 degrees in the signs Libra, Sagittarius, Aries or Cancer the person is likely to suffer badly. We will add here an example chart.

Example Chart 8

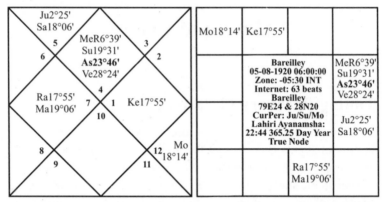

In this Cancer rising chart the ascending degree is 23.46 while Venus is at 28.24 degrees in Cancer. This person had a fall in January, 2014, and his wife had severe pain problem which was not going even after treatment. In January, 2014, transit Saturn was at 26 degrees and had been influencing the natal ascendant and Venus placed in the ascendant. Both husband and wife were suffering from health problem. In February, 2014, when transit Jupiter in Gemini came under the exact influence of natal Rahu the person had another fall and was hospitalized for four days for orthopedic surgery. The pain and troubled continued. The person was suggested astral remedies for Saturn, Rahu, Ketu and Jupiter. The person was advised that few months are going to be difficult for him and he should exercise patience and care.

To analyze recovery of the patient the horoscope is a must. Fairly accurate analysis can be made from a horary (prasna) chart, as well. The duration of recovery is worked out through the study of current sub-period and the separating functional malefic transit influences. When the slow moving functional malefic planets like Rahu-Ketu, Saturn and Jupiter exercising affliction(s) are stationary or taking more time in influencing a particular degree, the duration of the critical condition of the patient is generally longer. The pace of recovery depends upon the general strength of the planets in the natal chart and transit.

In this regard we have to proceed with the analysis in a systematic manner. Firstly, we have to work out the natal chart of the patient or one of the close relatives of the patient. In the absence of the birth particulars of the patient the analysis can be made from the horary chart or the chart of a close relative of the patient. After working out the chart, identify the slow moving functional malefic planet exerting malefic influence in the chart currently. That is to say we have to see the affliction in transit and/or the slow moving planet under functional malefic natal influence. Rahu and Ketu work in a malefic manner for all the ascendants. Identify the functional malefic planet(s) causing the serious condition and the strength of the natal position of the afflicted planet/house. After that find out if the affliction is on the most effective point of a house ruled by a weak planet or on a weak natal planet. The transit strength of the identified weak and afflicted planet should also be identified. The weakness of the Moon or ascendant in the natal chart makes the transit afflictions sensitive for the person. If the sub-period of a natal functional benefic is running, the results may not be serious and the recovery depends on the separation of the functional malefic influence on the weak natal/transit positions. While the seriousness may go when the separating influence is one degree longitude apart, the recovery may be possible when the separating effect is five degrees longitude apart between the afflicting planet and the afflicted planet/house. The general strong position of transit planets hastens the recovery while the weak position delays the same. The brightness/ strength of the Moon is a significant factor for consideration and transit affliction of the Moon gives the possible timing of set-backs indicating deterioration in condition. The brief spells of transit affliction of the Moon can be avoided for major medical remedies like starting of a new medication, operation, etc. to avoid immediate complications in the treatment.

For the benefit of the readers, we would now take up some illustrations so that the readers can comprehend the application of a systematic approach. The first three charts of this chapter pertain to serious indoor patients in the second fortnight of February, 1995. The general planetary position was not encouraging besides it being a dark half. Mars was in its sign of debilitation. The Sun was weak as its dispositor was weak and the Sun was under the close aspect of Rahu. Saturn was combust; Venus changed the sign and underwent the state of old age and infancy. Jupiter was weak due to its being in the debilitated navamsa. The general weakness of majority of the planets kept the pace of recovery of patients quite slow and the transit afflictions of the Sun and the Moon increased intensity of seriousness.

Chart 10

Male born 14th October 1929, 2306 Hrs. 74E18 31N35, India.

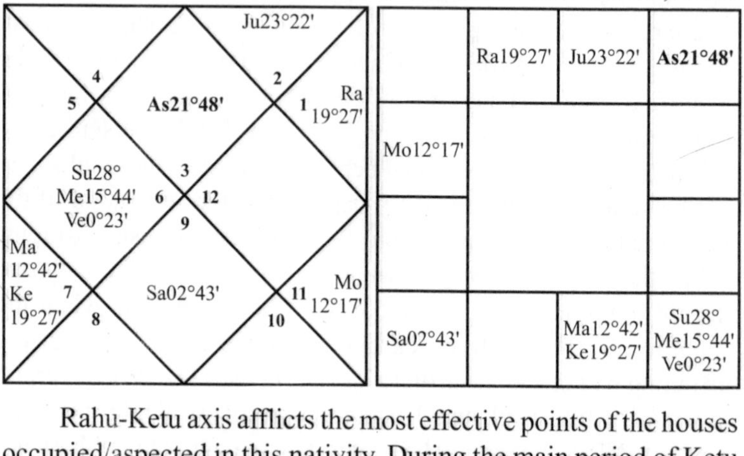

	Ju23°22'		
4 / 5 As21°48'	2 / 1 Ra 19°27'		
Su28° Me15°44' Ve0°23' 3 / 6 / 12 / 9			
Ma 12°42' Ke 7 19°27' 8 Sa02°43'	11 / 10 Mo 12°17'		

	Ra19°27'	Ju23°22'	As21°48'
Mo12°17'			
Sa02°43'		Ma12°42' Ke19°27'	Su28° Me15°44' Ve0°23'

Rahu-Ketu axis afflicts the most effective points of the houses occupied/aspected in this nativity. During the main period of Ketu and the sub-period of Mars the functional malefic planets Rahu and Ketu, exercising close influence on the fifth house in the natal chart, came under their own transit influence and gave the problem of acidity and burning sensation in the food pipe. On 18th January, 1995, the transit Rahu formed close conjunction with natal Mars, who was in its sign of debilitation in transit. On 13th February, 1995, when the transit influence of Rahu and Ketu further intensified on natal Mars, the person was admitted to the hospital for an operation for removal of a suspected malignant growth in the food pipe to which the person succumbed on 6th March, 1995, when the transit malefic influence of Rahu and Ketu on weak natal Mars was continuing. The speed of Rahu was quite slow and it took the toll. The sub-period of Rahu was indicative of such an eventuality in the main period of Ketu which is the most malefic planet for the natives born under the ascending sign of Gemini.

Chart 11

Horary chart for 27th February, 1995, 1545 hrs. New Delhi, India.

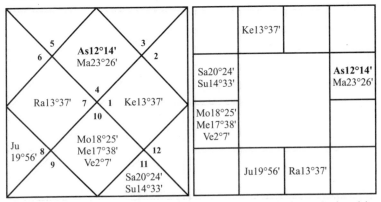

The query was regarding the illness of a relative admitted in the ICU. The horary chart was made. Rahu-Ketu axis was closely afflicting the most effective points of the houses occupied and aspected. The lord of the eighth house ruling death was severely afflicting the lord of the sixth house, Jupiter. The horary chart clearly indicated that the lord of the house of family is under the exact affliction of Rahu and was in the process of forming close conjunction with the lord of the eighth house in the eighth house. The conjunction of the lord of the second house ruling family was becoming further close with the lord of the eighth house and was also continuing under the close aspect of transit Rahu.

The lord of the ascendant of the horary chart was also entering the eighth house and coming under the close influence of Rahu indicating grief to the native. The patient died in the morning hours of the 1st March, 1995. The weak lord of the ascendant of the horary chart had also entered the eighth house and come under the close affliction of Rahu.

Appropriate astral remedies for the afflicting planets play a major role in toning down the severity of the afflictions. No astral remedies were being performed in this case.

During the second half of February, 1995, there were number of casualties in the ICU while the position of ICU patients reportedly started improving in the bright half and after the Sun was free from the close affliction of Rahu.

Chart 12

Male born 18th February 1952, 1630 hrs. New Delhi, India.

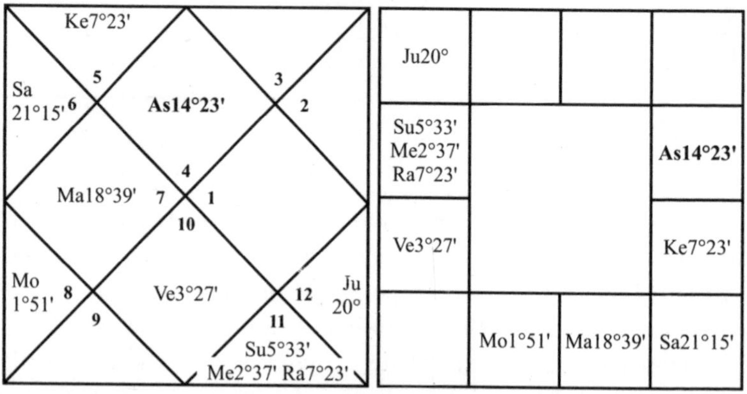

The lord of the ascendant is debilitated and in infancy. It is weak but well placed and unafflicted. Mars, the lord of the tenth house, closely aspects the tenth house which is a positive factor for the longevity in view of the weakness of the prime factor of longevity, the lord of the ascendant. The functional malefic planets, Saturn and Jupiter, closely aspect each other giving rise to possibility of death through serious illness or an accident. Jupiter rules the house of illness and Saturn rules the house of death. The Sun and combust Mercury are placed in the eighth house. The Sun is suffering from the close affliction of Rahu-Ketu axis. The Sun is the significator for the vitality. The planetary configurations clearly deny the full life span. The native had just completed 43 years of age. The native was admitted in the hospital for liver cirrhosis on 22nd February, 1995, and was in the sub-period of Saturn in the main period of Ketu. Jupiter is significator for liver. The sub-period was of a planet which is indicative of death. In transit, besides the Moon being in the dark half, the Sun was in the eighth house, Jupiter had formed close aspect with the natal position of Jupiter. Rahu / Ketu axis was afflicting the most effective point of the eighth house. Rahu and Ketu were afflicting the most effective points of the houses occupied and aspected. Transit Saturn was exactly afflicting transit Jupiter. It was considered that the recovery of the patient was almost impossible. The patient breathed his last, four days later, when the transit Sun came under the exact aspect of Rahu.

Chart 13

Male born 7th July 1994, 0705 hrs. 73E47 18N57 India.

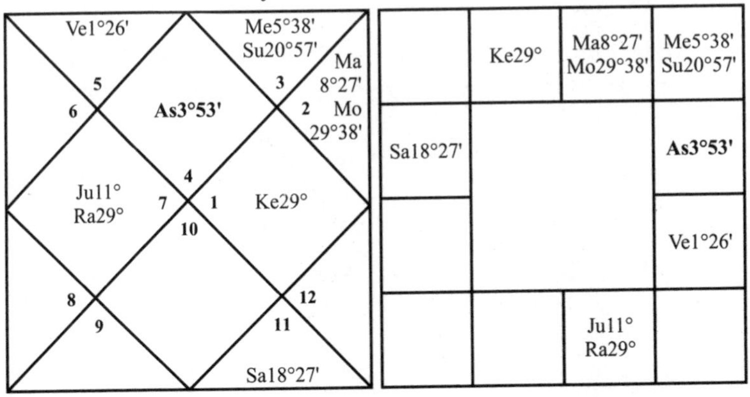
Ve1°26'
Me5°38'
Su20°57'
Ma 8°27'
Mo 29°38'
As3°53'
Ju11°
Ra29°
Ke29°
Sa18°27'
1
2
3
4
5
6
7
8
9
10
11
12
Ke29°
Ma8°27'
Mo29°38'
Me5°38'
Su20°57'
Sa18°27'
As3°53'
Ve1°26'
Ju11°
Ra29°

The lord of the ascendant is in its sign of exaltation and unafflicted but very weak as it is in the state of extreme old age. The lord of the eighth house is strong and not creating any close affliction in the chart. In this way it strengthens the longevity and indicates gains to father but causes obstructions and ill health during its sub-period. Mercury and the Sun are badly placed but do not suffer from any close affliction. The functional malefic Jupiter, too, does not cause any close affliction in the chart. The child was reported to be suffering seriously from meningitis since 21st November, 1994. The native was running the sub-period of Mercury in the main period of Mars. The sub-period of a weak functional benefic planet was not considered to be dangerous for life. Transit Jupiter was afflicting the most effective point of the fifth house and the most effective point of the houses aspected, as well. Simultaneously, the transit Rahu had also formed close aspect with natal Sun and Saturn placed in the twelfth and eighth houses, respectively. Transit aspects were separating towards the end of the year 1994. Therefore, native's parents were advised for propitiatory measures for Rahu and Jupiter and strengthening measures for the weak functional benefic planets through the use of a Kavach (Amulet). The native responded to treatment completely by the end of December, 1994.

Chart 14

Male born 25th March 1981, 1728 hrs. New Delhi, India.

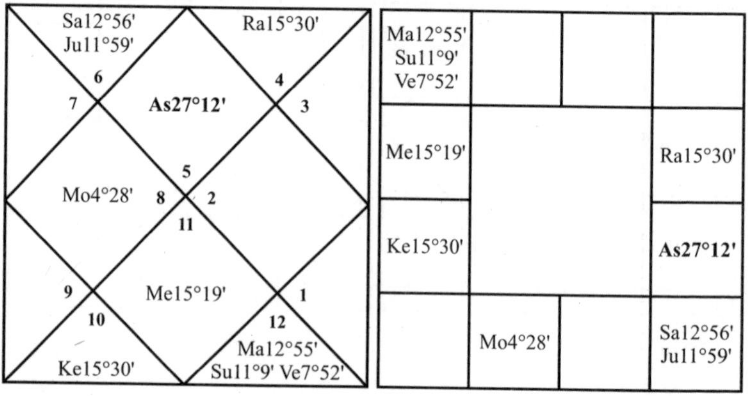

Ma12°55' Su11°9' Ve7°52'			
Me15°19'			Ra15°30'
Ke15°30'			As27°12'
	Mo4°28'		Sa12°56' Ju11°59'

The lord of the ascendant is badly placed in the eighth house in close conjunction with the functional benefic planets, Mars and Venus. The Sun and Mars suffer from the close affliction of Rahu from the twelfth house. The Moon occupies its sign of debilitation.

Saturn and Jupiter are well placed and are closely conjunct with each other but both of them suffer from the close aspect of Ketu from the sixth house. Mercury is also well placed planet but its dispositor is badly afflicted. The sub-period of Rahu robbed the courage of the native due to affliction of Rahu to the Sun and the combust Mars and the native developed fear phobia. The treatment from different sources proved to be of little help. On 25th of August, 1994, the astral counseling and remedies were sought. The native was suggested charities for Rahu, avoiding of the grey color clothes and the use of protective disk, Kavach, for strengthening of the weak functional benefic planets which proved helpful and indicated improvement in the general condition of the native. The full rehabilitation of the native was slow due to the following sub-periods of weak Jupiter and Saturn and as both of these planets were afflicted by Ketu by way of an aspect from the house of diseases.

Chart 15

Female born 15th December 1982, 0835 hrs. New Delhi, India.

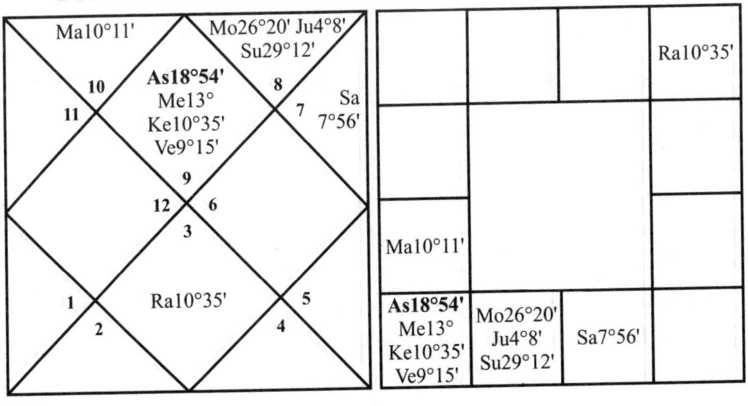

			Ra10°35'
	Ma10°11'		
As18°54' Me13° Ke10°35' Ve9°15'	Mo26°20' Ju4°8' Su29°12'	Sa7°56'	

North Indian chart:

- House 8: Mo26°20' Ju4°8' Su29°12'
- House 10/11: Ma10°11'
- As18°54' Me13° Ke10°35' Ve9°15' (House 9)
- House 7: Sa 7°56'
- House 5/4: Ra10°35'

The functional malefic planet, the Moon, is debilitated, badly placed and is closely afflicting the weak Sun. The lord of the ascendant is badly placed. Rahu-Ketu axis closely afflicts Mercury and Venus. Rahu closely afflicts Saturn. Mars is the only strong planet. Mars is in the sign of exaltation and does not suffer from any affliction. The weak ascendant lord and afflicted planets make a native prone to ill-health. During the end of sub-period of Mercury in the main period of Ketu the native suffered from loss of memory. The astral remedies were sought towards the end of 1994 after trying medical and psychiatric treatment of all types. As the disease had not been the result of the transit influence but is indicative due to the affliction of Mercury which is closely conjunct with Ketu, no short term treatment gave relief. The astral propitiatory remedies for Rahu, Ketu and the Moon together with a Kavach for strengthening the weak and afflicted functional benefic planets were suggested. The use of the astral remedies started giving improvement.

Chart 16

Male born 20th March 1992, 0734 hrs. New Delhi, India.

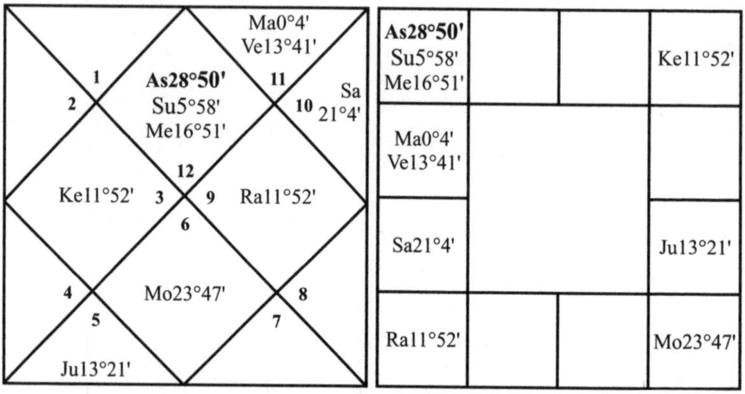
Ma0°4'
Ve13°41'
1
As28°50'
11
Sa
2
Su5°58'
10 21°4'
Me16°51'
12
Ke11°52' 3
9 Ra11°52'
6
4
Mo23°47'
8
5
7
Ju13°21'
As28°50'
Su5°58'
Me16°51'
Ke11°52'
Ma0°4'
Ve13°41'
Sa21°4'
Ju13°21'
Ra11°52'
Mo23°47'

No mooltrikona sign rises in the ascendant and therefore the lord of the eighth house governs the longevity. Mars is in extreme infancy and placed in the twelfth house. Badly placed Jupiter is closely afflicted by the aspects of Rahu and the most malefic planet,

Venus. Venus is closely afflicted by the aspect of the functional malefic planet, Ketu. Venus receives close aspect of the functional benefic, Jupiter, though it is of little help because of Jupiter's own bad placement and affliction. Mercury, the significator for speech and analytical power, is also weak due to debilitation & combustion.

Mars, the main period lord at birth, rules the second house which inter alia other things also rules speech. The weakness of both, the lord of the house of speech and the significator for speech and the affliction of lord of the twelfth house to the significator of speech, Mercury, have shown prominent results in this case. The native had almost no speech up to the middle of the year 1995 when the astral remedies were sought. In such cases, the astral remedies also have limitations in making significant improvement as none of the second house, its lord and Mercury has any beneficial impact on them nor is Jupiter strong.

Chart 17

Male born 15th July 1994, 1030 hrs 77E04 28N36, India.

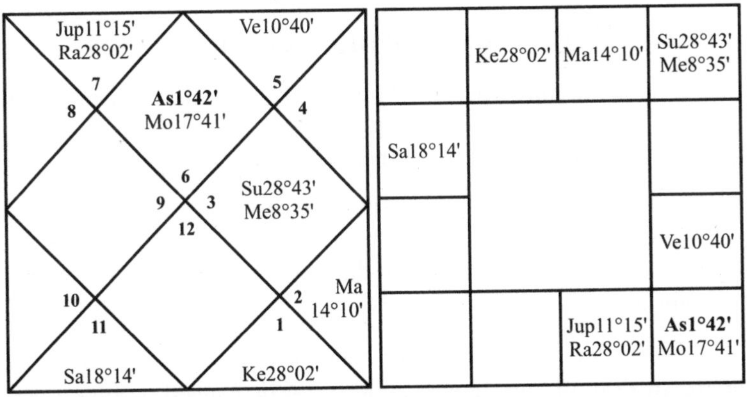

Rahu closely aspects and afflicts the weak Sun. The most malefic planet, Mars, closely aspects badly placed Venus. Rahu-Ketu axis afflicts the most effective points of the ninth, eleventh, first, third, fifth and seventh houses. Similarly, the Sun afflicts the most effective points of the eleventh and fifth houses, in the nativity.

The Moon, Mercury, Mars and Saturn are strong in this birth chart. At birth the native was running the sub-period of Saturn in the main period of the Moon. Saturn rules the sixth house and protects the health as it is strong. The native was suffering from jaundice at birth. However, the sickness at birth was given by the close affliction of Rahu to the Sun which separated only in the end of August, 1994. Whenever, there is exact affliction of the functional malefic planets to the most effective point of houses, the sub-period of a functional malefic is running at birth and the functional malefic being a slow moving planet is stationary or having a slower motion, the native suffers from ill health right at birth. If the prime significator for longevity is not weak, badly placed and afflicted, as in this case, the native recovers from the sickness prevailing at the time of birth as soon as the functional malefic planet's close conjunction with the afflicted planet separates. The natal and transit position of the planets at birth is same and the transit movement of functional malefic planets over the natal position of afflicted planets helps in arriving at the conclusions.

Timing Return of Missing Persons

This is another area in which no other science is helpful. A person may be missing due to variety of reasons. It may be a willful absence or involuntary absence. The willful absence may be because of emotional involvement, fear psyche or because of some difference of opinion. The involuntary disappearance may be because of illness on the way, abduction or problems with means of communications.

Such type of questions are handled through prasna (horary) charts or through birth charts. These can be caused by functional malefic transit influences both on natal or prasna (horary) charts. The influence of the nodes (Rahu-Ketu) is more pertinent. The timing is done with the help of the separating transit influences. When the functional malefic transit influences are on other transit planets, the separating impact is faster compared to the stationary transit influence on the weak natal planets. The transit functional malefic influence is seen on the most effective points of the ascendant, third house, fourth house, fifth house, seventh house or the tenth house or their lords. The malefic influence caused by Ketu, functional malefic planet Mars and the lords of the sixth and eighth houses on the ascendant or its lord or any other weak and badly placed planet results in involuntary disappearance while the involvement of Rahu, lords of the third, fifth, seventh and twelfth houses may cause willful disappearance.

For obtaining information of whereabouts, we see when the significator planets of the information, that is the Moon, Mercury or the lord of the third house, create influence on the third house, the planets placed therein or the ascendant. The other important factor to be kept in view is the speed of the planets in transit. The slow speed or stationary position of planets delays the return while the fast speed hastens the separation effect and results in early return/ information.

The issue will be discussed further with the help of case studies.

Chart 18

Female born 20th August 1983, 0525 hrs. New Delhi, India.

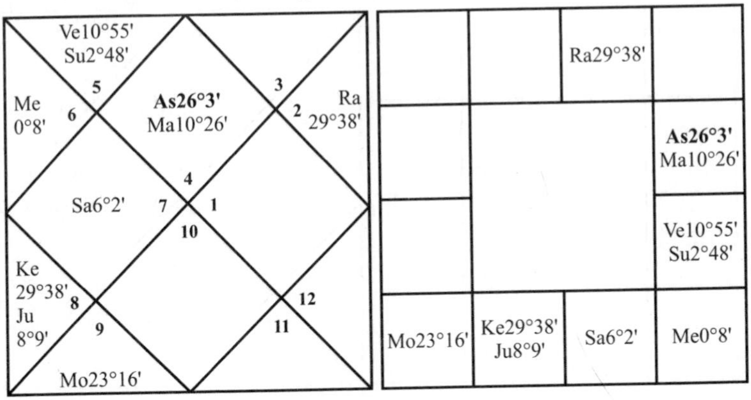

		Ra29°38'	
			As26°3' Ma10°26'
			Ve10°55' Su2°48'
Mo23°16'	Ke29°38' Ju8°9'	Sa6°2'	Me0°8'

The native left home on 29th November, 1996, in the early morning. The prasna chart was made on 30th November, 1996, at 2140 hours at Gurgaon.

The strong Moon in the ascendant of the prasna chart prepared indicated that the native was physically fit. In the natal chart Mars ruling the tenth house, is placed in the ascendant and the same is under the close influence of the functional malefic planets, Jupiter and Saturn. The influence of lord of the eighth house on the lord of the tenth house and the close influence of Rahu to most effective points of the third, fifth and seventh houses make the person interested in carnal pleasures and impels for acting as per one's own will. At the time of leaving the house, the native was running the sub-period of Rahu in the main period of the Moon. The transit Mercury was under the influence of natal Rahu-Ketu in the fifth house. The sub-period of Mercury in the main period of Mercury was operating in the prasna chart. As the transit Mercury was under the influence of natal Rahu and in the prasna chart its sub-period was in operation, Mercury was picked up for timing the event of return. It was indicated that the native will return around 8th of December, 1996, when the transit Mercury would have cleared from the transit influence of Saturn, the lord of the eighth house in the prasna chart. However, it was also thought that the information might well be received around 4th December, 1996, when transit Moon conjoins the natal Mercury in the third house. The native rang up on the night of 4th December, 1996, and returned on 8th December, 1996. In this case the involvement of Mars gave willful movements. Whenever the most effective point of the fifth house, third house, Venus and the lords of the fifth or third houses are under the close impact of Rahu, it gives uncontrolled urges for carnal pleasures.

Chart 19

Horary chart for 15th November 1994, 1901 hrs. 28N27 77E01, India.

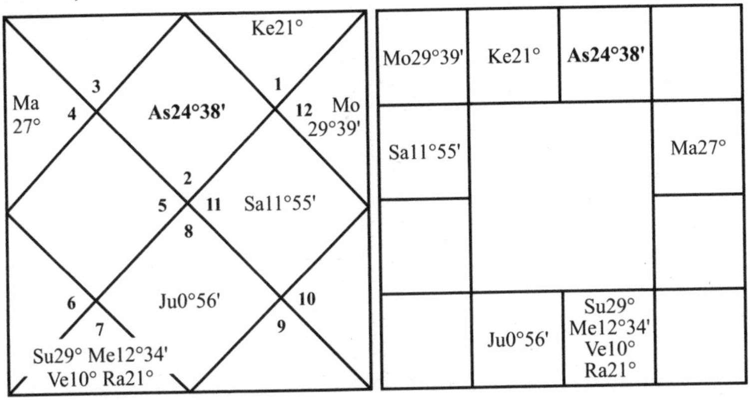
Ke21°
3
1
Ma 27°
4
As24°38'
12 Mo 29°39'
2
5
11
Sa11°55'
8
6
Ju0°56'
10
7
9
Su29° Me12°34'
Ve10° Ra21°
Mo29°39'
Ke21°
As24°38'
Sa11°55'
Ma27°
Ju0°56'
Su29°
Me12°34'
Ve10°
Ra21°

The lord of the eighth is conjunct with the lord of the fourth house. The lord of the fifth house is under the close influence of Venus. The most effective point of the third house and the weak lord of the fourth house are under the influence of Mars, the lord of the twelfth house. This girl left home on 7th November, 1994. On that day, the transit Jupiter was exerting its malefic influence on the Sun, the lord of the fourth house. The fourth house rules the character while the eighth house rules the carnal pleasures.

In this case, the Moon was considered as the significator for returning and the return was indicated when either the Moon transited the ascendant or the third house as the afflicting influence of Jupiter over the Sun had ceased to exist. The native returned on 20th November, 1994, when the Moon was close to the most effective point of the ascendant.

Chart 20

Female born 27th May 1970, 2200 hrs. Ahmedabad, India.

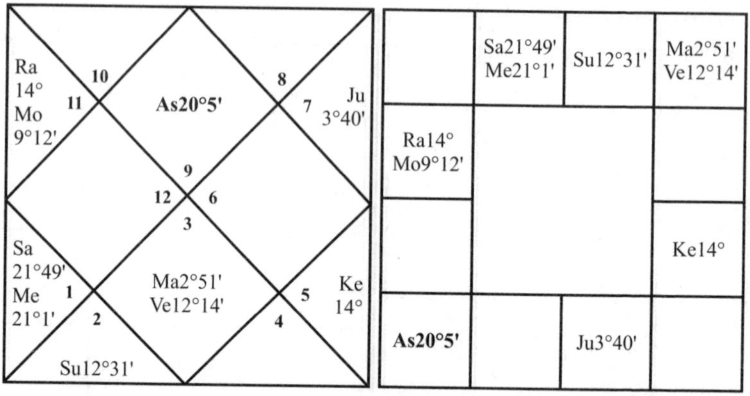

		Sa21°49' Me21°1'	Su12°31'	Ma2°51' Ve12°14'
Ra14° Mo9°12'				
				Ke14°
As20°5'			Ju3°40'	

The native disappeared on 8th December, 1994, when her marriage was fixed for the 22nd January, 1995. The lord of the third house is in close conjunction with the planet, Mercury, and both of these planets are placed in the fifth house, ruling emotions. Mercury is indicative of exercising one's choice as it rules the tenth house. Its association with the third lord in the house of emotions is indicative of strong emotional involvement. When the marriage was fixed by parents without her consent she eloped. In this case, transit Venus was under the close impact of natal Rahu and transit Saturn was under the close influence of natal Rahu. Transit Rahu was influencing natal Mercury and Saturn. She was running the sub-period of Venus in the main period of Jupiter. It was indicated that the native may return around 20th of January, 1995, when the close influence of transit Rahu would separate by about three to four degrees from the natal Saturn and Mercury. The native returned on 18th of January, 1995.

Chart 21

Male born 25th June 1946, 1325 hrs. 75E12, 31N49, India.

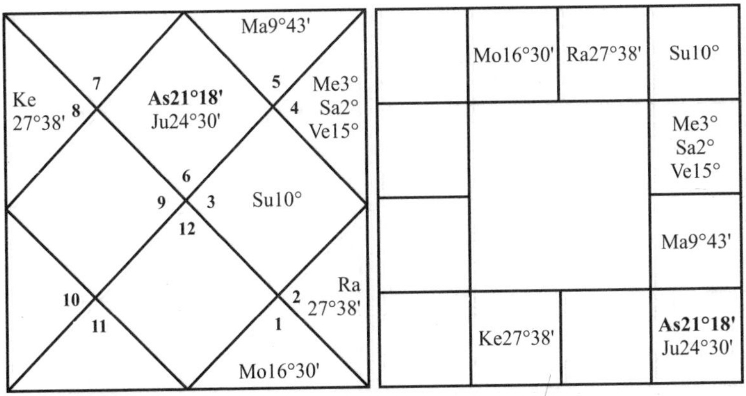

	Mo16°30'	Ra27°38'	Su10°
			Me3° Sa2° Ve15°
			Ma9°43'
	Ke27°38'		As21°18' Ju24°30'

(South Indian style diagram, left):
Ma9°43' (top), Me3° Sa2° Ve15° (house 4/5), Ke27°38' (house 7/8), As21°18' Ju24°30' (house 6), Su10° (house 3/12), Ra27°38' (house 1/2), Mo16°30' (bottom). Houses numbered 1–12.

The lord of the sixth house closely afflicts the lord of the ascendant. Rahu closely aspects the lord of the fourth house, Jupiter, placed in the ascendant. This person did not reach home after leaving his office on 24th November, 1994. A member of his family asked me about him on 25th November, 1994 at 0852 hours at Gurgaon. The transit Mercury was in Libra at 28 degrees and unafflicted. This meant he was alive. The transit Rahu was on the most effective point of the second house. As it had already crossed the natal degree of the ascendant, there was no other transit affliction and the transit Rahu was in its last phase of stationary movement. It was indicated that the native may return in a couple of days.

The native had fainted on 24th November, 1994 after leaving his office on the way and was hospitalized. The native returned home on the 28th November, 1994.

Chart 22

Horary chart for 23rd April 1995, 2145 hrs. New Delhi, India.

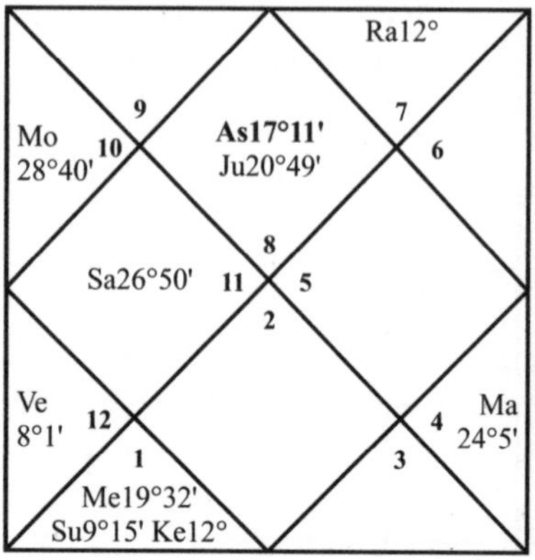
Ra12°
9
7
Mo
28°40'
10
As17°11'
Ju20°49'
6
8
Sa26°50'
11
5
2
Ve
8°1'
12
4
Ma
24°5'
1
3
Me19°32'
Su9°15' Ke12°

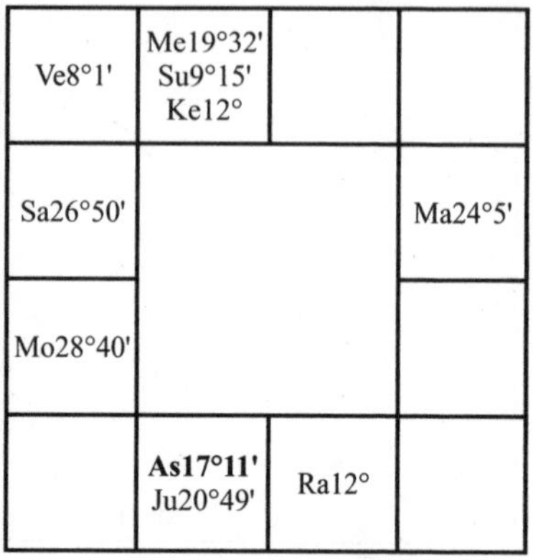
Ve8°1'
Me19°32'
Su9°15'
Ke12°
Sa26°50'
Ma24°5'
Mo28°40'
As17°11'
Ju20°49'
Ra12°

The native left home on 22nd April, 1995. Her engagement finalized in December, 1993, had broken after one year in the beginning of 1995. In the horary chart the functional malefic Mars afflicts the Moon causing mental and emotional disturbance. Jupiter and Saturn are well placed but weak in the chart and at the time of her disappearance she was running the sub-period of Saturn in the main period of Mars. The Sun was in conjunction with Ketu and Saturn was under the close affliction of Mars. As there was no planet in the eighth house and there is no mooltrikona sign in the eighth house, it was indicated that physically she was alright and was likely to return in a week's time. The conjunction of the Sun with Ketu was to separate and the Moon was to aspect the ascendant after a week. Mercury was also moving to the seventh house.

In her natal chart the Leo rises with Moon, the most malefic planet aspecting the most effective point of the fifth house from the eleventh house and with conjunction of the Sun and Mercury in the sixth house. That explains the reasons for the broken engagement. The native returned on 27th April, 95 when the Moon was on the MEP of the fifth house.

Chart 23

Female born 5th May 1980, 1014 hrs. 74E50 24N18, India.

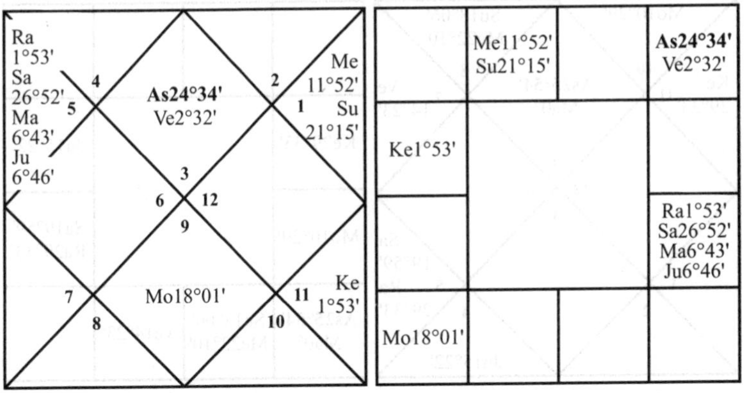
Ra 1°53'
Sa 26°52'
Ma 6°43'
Ju 6°46'
As24°34'
Ve2°32'
Me 11°52'
Su 21°15'
Mo18°01'
Ke 1°53'
1
2
3
4
5
6
7
8
9
10
11
12
Me11°52'
Su21°15'
As24°34'
Ve2°32'
Ke1°53'
Ra1°53'
Sa26°52'
Ma6°43'
Ju6°46'
Mo18°01'

Ketu afflicts Venus, Mars and Jupiter in the natal chart. The conjunction of Mars with Jupiter, lord of the seventh house, together with influence of Rahu on both of these planets in the house of initiative shows the initiative regarding marriage. The aspect of the lord of the third house on the most effective point of the fifth house is a supportive factor in this regard.

The transit Jupiter was in conjunction with the natal Moon on 12th July, 1996. At the time of question on 16th July, 1996, (with 17° ascendant rising in the sign Capricorn), the close influence of Rahu on the most effective point of the fifth house of the horary chart had started separating and it was predicted that the native may return before 20th of July, 1996. The native returned on 18th July, 1996.

Chart 24

Male born 4th December 1978, 0946 hrs. 76E38 27N34, India.

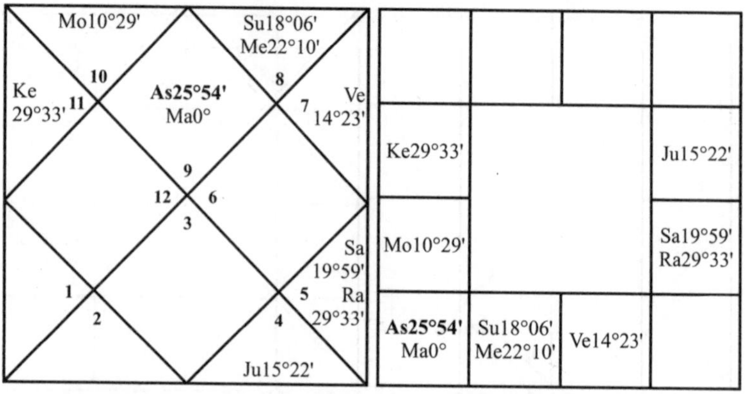

			Ke29°33'			Ju15°22'

(chart diagrams)

South Indian chart:

Ke29°33'			Ju15°22'
Mo10°29'			Sa19°59' Ra29°33'
As25°54' Ma0°	Su18°06' Me22°10'	Ve14°23'	

North Indian chart contents:
- Mo10°29' (house 10), Ke 29°33' (house 11)
- As25°54' Ma0°, Su18°06' Me22°10' (house 8), Ve14°23' (house 7)
- Sa19°59' Ra29°33' (house 5)
- Ju15°22'

The lord of the fifth house is extremely weak. Rahu afflicts the most effective point of the ascendant, third and fifth houses. This is indicative of weak intelligence and interest in loafing and pleasure seeking.

In October, 1992, when the transit Rahu afflicted natal Mars the native left home. The native was running the sub-period of weak and badly placed Mercury and was unemployed. Feeling sick of the constant reprimand of parents he left the home. The father was advised propitiatory astral remedies for Rahu and Ketu. The transit Rahu was becoming stationary at 27 degree in Dec' 92. Therefore, until it created a longitudinal difference of 5 degrees from the natal Mars, the return was not seen. The native returned home in the last week of March 1993.

Chart 25

Female born 8th November 1975, 1311 hrs. 77E08 28N37, India.

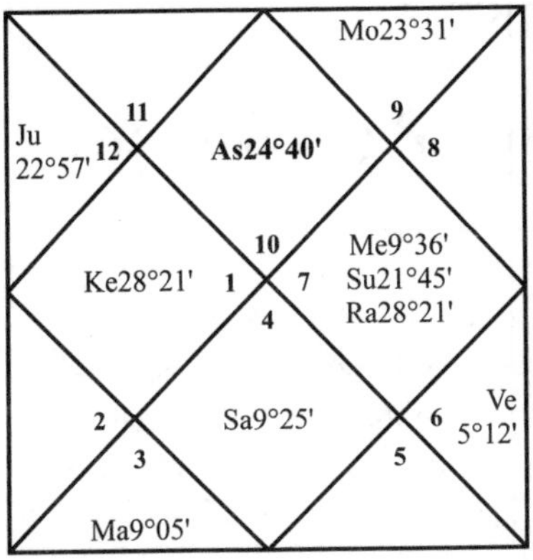
Mo23°31'
11
9
Ju
22°57'
12
As24°40'
8
10
Me9°36'
Su21°45'
Ra28°21'
Ke28°21'
1
7
4
Ve
5°12'
2
Sa9°25'
6
3
5
Ma9°05'

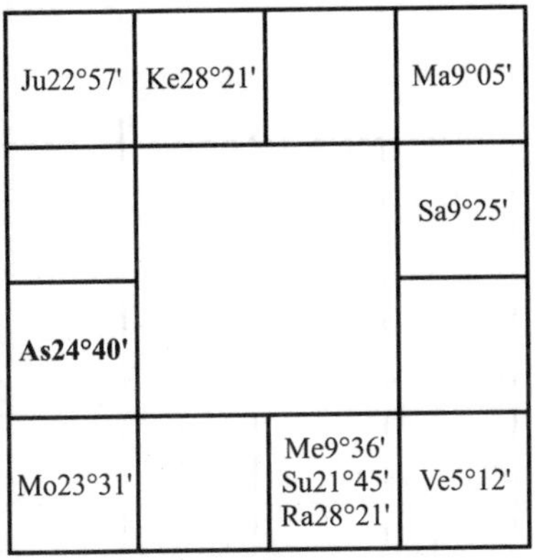
Ju22°57'
Ke28°21'
Ma9°05'
Sa9°25'
As24°40'
Mo23°31'
Me9°36'
Su21°45'
Ra28°21'
Ve5°12'

The most effective point of the fourth house is afflicted by the Sun, Rahu and Ketu. The lord of the twelfth house, Jupiter is debilitated in navamsa and is influencing the most effective point of the third house in a malefic manner. The influences on the third and fourth houses show the initiatives with regard to seeking physical relationship with the opposite sex represented by the lords of the eighth and twelfth houses. During the sub-period of Saturn in the main period of the Moon (ruling the house of family and the house of marriage, respectively) on 6th August, 1991, when Rahu was transiting the natal Moon in the twelfth house, the native left home.

The transit movement of Rahu was at a slow speed and it was indicated that the return may take about a month's time. The native returned on 10th of September, 1991, after a court marriage with a boy of her choice.

Chart 26

Male born 19th October 1974, 2210 hrs. 77E01 28N39, India.

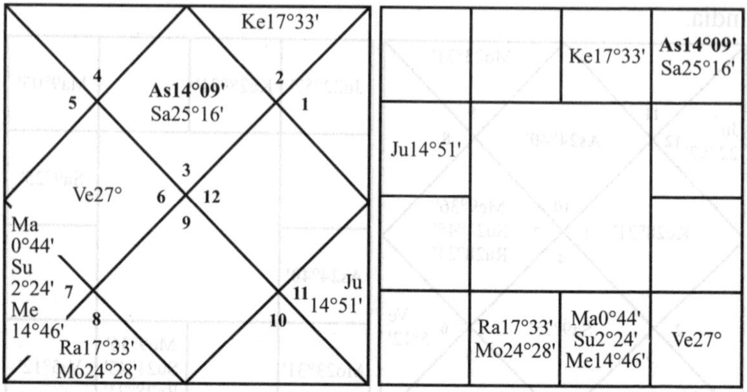

			Ke17°33'	As14°09' Sa25°16'
	Ju14°51'			
		Ra17°33' Mo24°28'	Ma0°44' Su2°24' Me14°46'	Ve27°

North Indian chart (left):

Ke17°33' (top)
As14°09' Sa25°16' (house with 4, 5, 2, 1)
Ve27° (6, 12, 3, 9)
Ma 0°44' Su 2°24' Me 14°46' (7, 8)
Ra17°33' Mo24°28'
Ju 14°51' (11, 10)

The weak lords of the third and eleventh houses are conjunct with each other in the fifth house. The debilitated Rahu afflicts the most effective point of the house of family from the sixth house by way of a close aspect. The lord of the seventh house, Jupiter, aspects the ascendant, third and the fifth houses and the Mercury placed in the fifth house closely. The debilitated lord of the second house is badly placed in the house of conflicts. The aspect of the lord of the seventh house ruling residence in distant or foreign places on the lord of the fourth house indicates movement to distant places. The native left home on 14th June, 1993, when he was running the sub-period of the Moon in the main period of Venus. Transit Rahu had formed close conjunction with natal Rahu.

Due to the affliction to the second house and bad placement of the weak Moon, the planets impelled a separation from the family due to disagreements on the ways he was conducting his life as a loafer. The prasna was made on 19th February, 1994, when he was still in the sub-period of the Moon running up to the end of 1995. The propitiatory remedial measures for Rahu were suggested to expedite the return. The information was received in the middle of

March 1994, while the native returned on 6th May, 1994. The transit Jupiter had formed auspicious conjunction with natal Mercury and was closely aspecting the natal Jupiter and the most effective point of ascendant. When the bad sub-period is running, a good transit influence is spotted for favorable results.

Chart 27

Horary chart for 15th January 1994, 1725 hrs. 77E08 28N37, India.

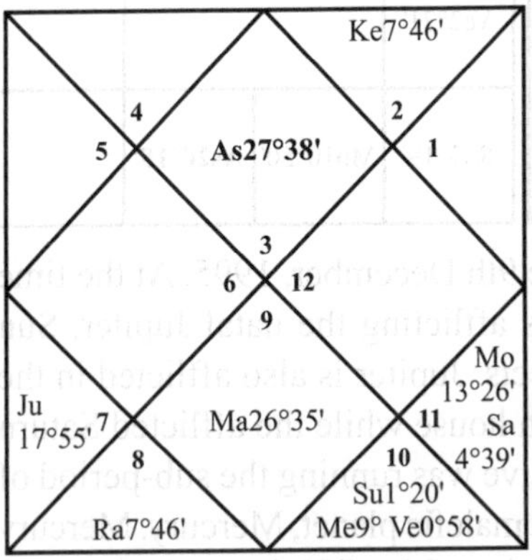

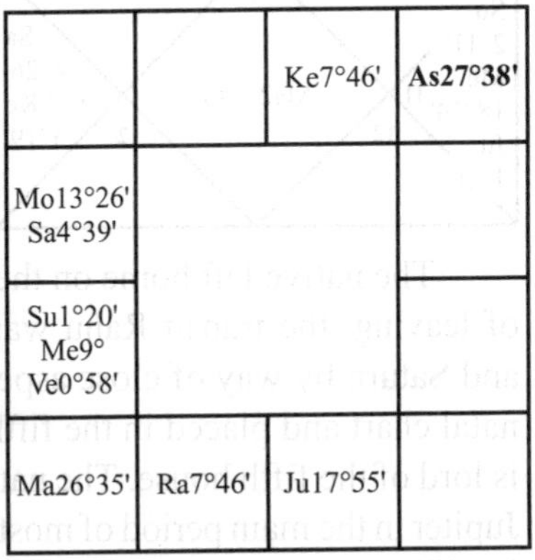

The lords of the third, fourth and fifth houses are placed in the eighth house and are weak. The Sun and Venus are in extreme infancy. These are indicative of poor education, lack of intelligence and careless attitude. During the sub-period of Mercury in the main period of Rahu as per the prasna chart when transit Mercury was under the exact influence of Ketu on 14th January, 1994, the native was reported missing. The prasna was made on 15th January, 1994, when the transit Mercury had already cleared by one degree from the affliction of aspect of Ketu. As the aspect of Mars to the most effective point of ascendant was going to be exact on the 17th January, 1994, it was predicted that the native may return on 17th or 18th January, 1994. The native returned on 18th January, 1994. The Mercury's longitudinal difference from the aspect of Ketu was five degrees.

Chart 28

Male born 15th February 1974, 0005 hrs. 77E08 28N37, India.

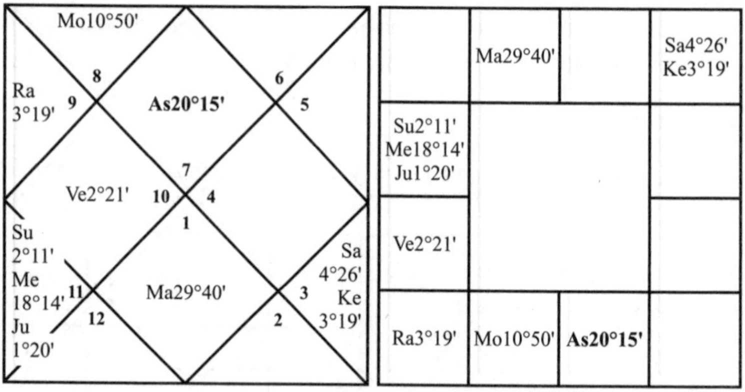
Mo10°50'
Ra 3°19'
9
8
As20°15'
6
5
7
Ve2°21'
10
4
1
Su 2°11'
Me 18°14'
Ju 1°20'
11
12
Ma29°40'
2
3
Sa 4°26'
Ke 3°19'
Ma29°40'
Sa4°26'
Ke3°19'
Su2°11'
Me18°14'
Ju1°20'
Ve2°21'
Ra3°19'
Mo10°50'
As20°15'

The native left home on the 9th December, 1995. At the time of leaving, the transit Rahu was afflicting the natal Jupiter, Sun and Saturn by way of close aspects. Jupiter is also afflicted in the natal chart and placed in the fifth house while the afflicted Saturn is lord of the fifth house. The native was running the sub-period of Jupiter in the main period of most malefic planet, Mercury. Mercury is afflicting the most effective point of the fifth house in the natal chart. The propitiatory remedies for Mercury, Rahu and Ketu were suggested, the performance of which resulted in return of the native in the middle of January, 1996, when the transit Rahu had separated by four and five degrees from the natal Jupiter and the Sun, respectively.

Chart 29

Male born 24th September 1966, 1000 hrs. 87E34 24N09, India.

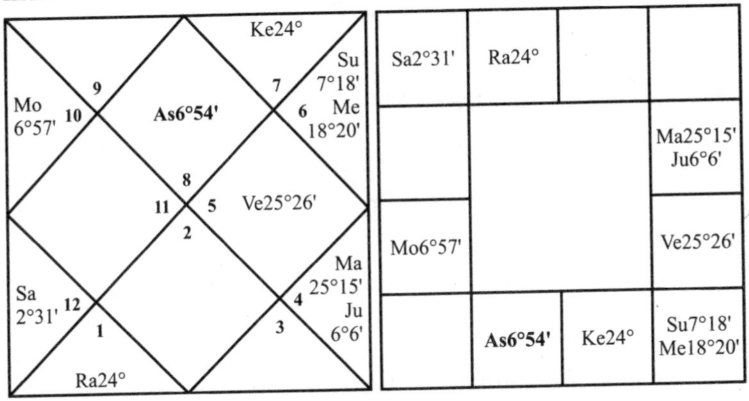
Ke24°
Su 7°18'
Me 18°20'
Mo 6°57'
As6°54'
Ve25°26'
Ma 25°15'
Ju 6°6'
Sa 2°31'
Ra24°
9
10
7
6
8
11
5
2
12
1
4
3
Sa2°31'
Ra24°
Ma25°15'
Ju6°6'
Mo6°57'
Ve25°26'
As6°54'
Ke24°
Su7°18'
Me18°20'

Mars, Venus, Rahu and Ketu are the functional malefic planets in this nativity. Venus, ruling the house of losses, is closely afflicted by the aspect of Rahu from the sixth house. The native incurred huge business losses involving borrowed capital in the sub-period of Ketu and beginning of the sub-period of Venus in the main period of Rahu. Ketu is placed in the house of losses. With the onset of the sub-period of Venus the losses multiplied and the fear of the native increased for loss of reputation and the pressure of financers. The native left home in February, 1997, when the transit Rahu and Ketu started afflicting his natal weak Sun, Moon, Jupiter and weak Saturn besides afflicting the most effective points of the houses transited and aspected. The severe affliction of Rahu to Venus in the sub-period of Venus in the main period of Rahu did not indicate early relief. The astral help was sought after four months of his disappearance in February, 1997. The propitiatory astral remedies were suggested to be performed by his wife. The propitiatory remedies resulted in the return of the native in December, 1997.

Chapter 5

Financial Prosperity Through Astral Remedies

Materialism is all pervading in this world. To satisfy their desires, human beings need finances. This makes the study of the sources of finance in a nativity one of the important aspects of the interpretation of a horoscope. One's satisfactory financial position enables one to control basic human instincts of greed, anger, pride, lust, etc, and generates positive personality traits like kindness, honesty, sincerity, benevolence, contentment, etc. A contented person is in a position to progress physically, intellectually, morally and spiritually. Progress enables the optimum use of an individual's life. The conservation, protection and promotion of good human values results in the progress of nations and humanity as a whole. **In Kaliyuga, one who controls the basic instincts viz. greed, anger, pride and lust besides performing his duties sincerely and honestly, is considered to be in the service of God.** This shows how important the study of the financial position is in a nativity and the approach to enhance the financial prospects.

To analyze the financial prospects of a person from the horoscope, we look for the strength of the Moon and Jupiter being significators for finance and the strength of Venus ruling luxuries. Besides these planets, we look for (1) the lords of those houses which contain mooltrikona signs, (2) the houses ruling finance, that is the 1st, 2nd, 3rd, 5th, 8th, 10th and 11th houses, which contain mooltrikona sign and the strength of the lords of these houses, (3) the close conjunctions and aspects of various planets to the above mentioned houses and planets, (4) the planets placed in the houses signifying financial gains.

Now, we take up the approach to analyze the sources of financial gains, the reasons for financial strains and astral remedies for augmenting financial gains.

Besides dhanakaraka (significators of wealth), the operating planetary periods of the lords of the houses which contain mooltrikona signs indicate the sources of finance - be it through inheritance, business, service, investments, etc. The strong natal planets (when strong in transit, too) generate good finances during the course of their operating periods. When the dhanakaraka, acting as a functional malefic, forms close conjunction/aspect with other planets or the most effective point of any house, instead of being helpful it would be detrimental for growth.

A strong lord of the first house, depending upon the planet, gives good finances through initiative and drive. The Sun and the Moon indicate executive posts with the State/Government while Mercury and Venus indicate financial gains through business ventures including trading. Mars and Saturn involve one in manufacturing industries/production units. Jupiter engages one in the service of state as a professional adviser in the fields of law and finance or as a practicing lawyer or a Chartered Accountant or an astrologer. The strong support of Mercury is further helpful. Hereafter, we refer to the lords of various houses being strong or well placed. 'Well placed' would indicate placed in any of the houses except the sixth, eighth and twelfth houses. The lord of the second house containing a mooltrikona sign gives financial gains through status, investments and family wealth. Similarly, the lord of the third house indicates financial gains through the fields of communications, publications, marketing and through entrepreneurial activities.

The lord of the fourth house indicates gains through business in the fields of items of luxury-including properties and vehicles, hotel management and education. The lord of the fifth house gives financial gains through work in teaching, training and development organizations, research organizations, managerial positions, etc. The lord of the sixth house when not afflicting any other natal planetary position or the most effective point of a house gives financial gains through legal, financial and medical professions. The lord of the seventh house indicates gains through partnership business, business or professional ventures abroad, the items of luxury, import-export and trading- especially in the fields of cosmetics and exclusive items of personal grooming. The lord of the eighth house, without causing any affliction, when strong, gives easy gains, gains through inheritance, winning in the games of chances and gains through draw of lots. The lord of the ninth house blesses with financial gains through parental wealth and status, working in religious/spiritual organizations and working with export-import organizations. The lord of the tenth house gives executive status with the state or business when the concerned planets are fairly strong. The lord of the eleventh house gives gains through elder brothers, gains through friends and gains through the signification of the houses where the lord of the eleventh house is placed. The strong and unafflicting lord of the twelfth house gives financial gains in foreign lands and through the business of luxury items.

If the significator planets are weak, even if they take the person to the business/profession/service indicated by these planets, or the significations of a particular house, the results would be modest and will cause financial strains. Weak planets, when afflicted by the functional malefic planets, cause severe financial strains. The close involvement of the Sun indicates big operations.

The subject will be discussed further through case studies given hereunder:

Chart 30

Male born 22nd April 1950, 0315 Hrs. 80E53 16N02, India.

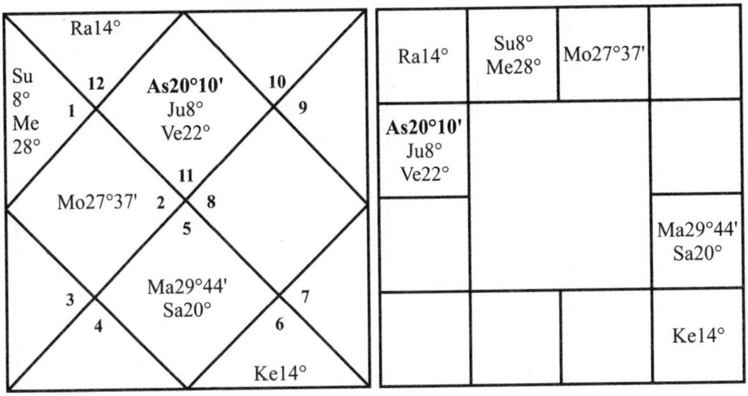
Ra14°
Su 8° Me 28°
As20°10'
Ju8°
Ve22°
Mo27°37'
Ma29°44'
Sa20°
Ke14°
12
1
10
9
11
2
8
5
3
4
7
6
Ra14°
Su8° Me28°
Mo27°37'
As20°10'
Ju8°
Ve22°
Ma29°44'
Sa20°
Ke14°

The first, eleventh, third, eighth and ninth houses ruling financial matters contain the mooltrikona signs. Therefore, besides the wealth giving planet, Saturn, Jupiter, Mars, Mercury and Venus become significators for financial prosperity. All the planets are well placed. Saturn and Venus aspect each other closely. The close influence of Venus on the ascendant and the lord of ascendant made the native an expert in the field of management and law. At a young age, the native worked at very senior levels and could draw the highest possible remuneration. The real boom came in the sub-period of Venus in the main period of Saturn as both of these planets are functional benefic planets and are well placed in the nativity. The native earned through foreign lands, as well. To ward off the possibility of transit affliction to these planets, the native was advised to wear a Kavach in an auspicious time and perform propitiatory astral remedies for the Moon, Mercury, Rahu and Ketu. The weakness of Mars, the lord of the house of initiatives, and Mercury, being the most malefic planet, in the house of initiatives, did not allow the native to venture into his own business despite his excellent professional competence.

Chart 31

Male born in February 1965.

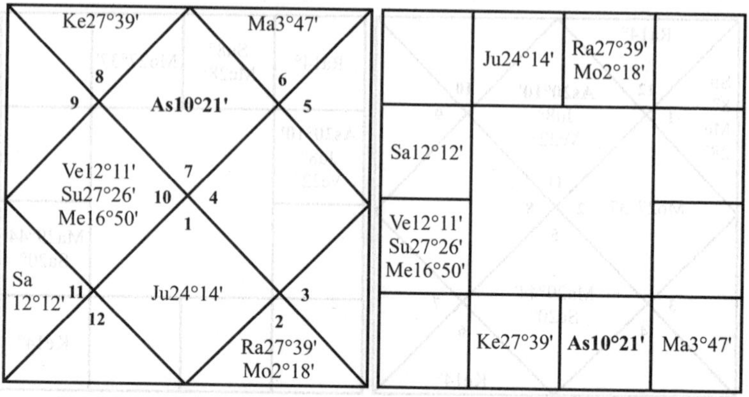

Ke27°39'		Ma3°47'	

Chart (South Indian style):

	Ju24°14'	Ra27°39' Mo2°18'	
Sa12°12'			
Ve12°11' Su27°26' Me16°50'			
	Ke27°39'	As10°21'	Ma3°47'

Chart (North Indian / diamond style):
- Ke27°39' (house 8, 9)
- Ma3°47' (house 6, 5)
- As10°21' (house 7)
- Ve12°11', Su27°26', Me16°50' (house 10, 1)
- Sa12°12' (house 11, 12)
- Ju24°14' (house 3, 2)
- Ra27°39', Mo2°18' (house 2)

In this nativity, besides dhanakaraka, the Moon, Jupiter and Venus also become significators together with the Sun and Saturn. Venus is strongly placed in the chart and closely aspects the most effective point of the tenth house. The well placed Sun, ruling the house of income, is under the close influence of Rahu from the eighth house. Rahu not only makes a person manipulative but also gives courage to defy all social and governmental norms. The affliction of the Sun robs him of happiness from father, friends and does not bless the native with an elder brother. The benefits drawn in the sub-period of Rahu are generally lost in the sub-period of planets under their exact influence. Such a planetary position gives heart problems at a young age and lots of persistent anxiety. The weak Saturn occupies its own mooltrikona sign and is close to the most effective point and promotes affairs of the second, fifth, seventh and eleventh houses i.e. the houses occupied and aspected. The native made an industrial kingdom in the sub-periods of Jupiter and Saturn in the main period of Rahu. Jupiter rules the house of initiatives and is well placed and the good placement of Saturn has already been explained above. The weak lord of the tenth house i.e. the Moon as also the Sun, Saturn and Jupiter required strengthening for which the native was provided with a Kavach. The native was also advised to wear a pearl and a ruby.

Chart 32

Male born 11th October 1960.

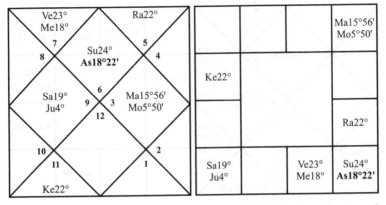

The fairly strong placement of the eighth lord confers good gains through inheritance i.e. indicates a sound financial position of the father. The Sun is also well placed. The lord of the ascendant is posited in the second house exactly near the most effective point and indicates a very good status in life through self-efforts besides the role of the lord of the house of inheritance, Mars. The lord of the second house is also well placed in the second house, itself. Jupiter and the Moon closely aspect each other and are indicative of long-lived parents and gains of property. The close influence of Mars on the tenth house, on the ascendant and on Saturn gave hot temperament and puts obstructions in the smooth progress. The close mutual aspect of Saturn and Mars indicates the incidence of disputes in the matters of inheritance and goodwill. Such a planetary configuration makes a man short tempered and aggressive in behaviour. The close aspect of Ketu from the sixth house to natal Venus, ruling the house of status, threatens the status with conflicts / litigation. The native is the managing director of a big industrial group and was advised astral remedies to ward off the evil influences of the functional malefic planets, the Sun, Saturn, Mars, Rahu and Ketu.

Chart 33

Male born 17th June 1942 1450 Hrs., 74E44 30N40, India.

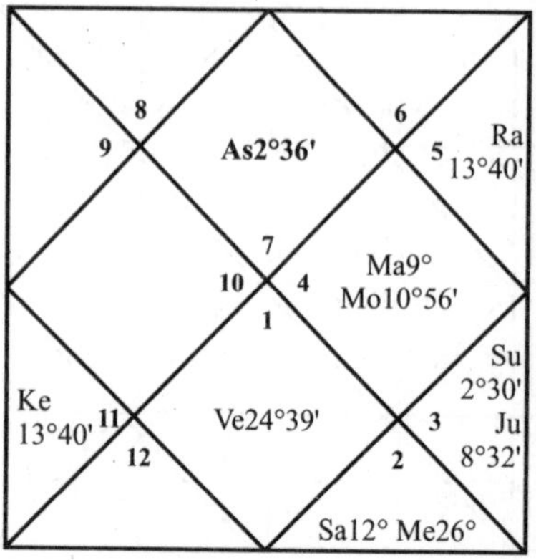
8
9
As2°36'
6
5
Ra 13°40'
7
10
4
1
Ma9° Mo10°56'
Su 2°30'
Ke 13°40'
11
12
Ve24°39'
3
Ju 8°32'
2
Sa12° Me26°

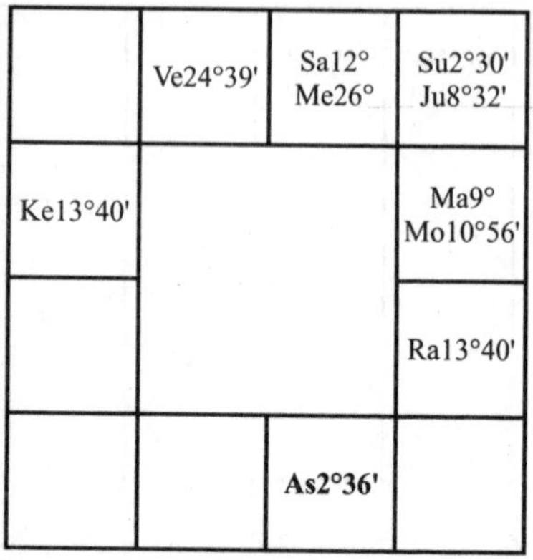
Ve24°39'
Sa12° Me26°
Su2°30' Ju8°32'
Ke13°40'
Ma9° Mo10°56'
Ra13°40'
As2°36'

Besides dhanakaraka, the Moon, Venus and Jupiter also become significators of financial resources together with the Sun and Saturn. Coming from an average family, the native acquired good position as a general manager in a production unit and earned good sums of money in the sub-periods of well placed planets in the main period of Venus. Venus is well placed and unafflicted. The lord of the tenth house is strong and associated closely with the planet ruling factories, Mars. The Sun (though weak) and Jupiter are well placed in a Sun-like house. The lord of the fifth house, Saturn, closely aspects and promotes both the Moon and Mars to some extent. Jupiter blessed the native with good initiative and drive and its placement in the house of fortune made the native a self-made successful professional. The Sun, though weak, as the lord of eleventh house, in the house of fortune near the most effective point of the ninth house, bestowed gains through his professional ventures and highly placed friends.

Chart 34

Male born 20th June 1956, 1035 Hrs., 80E53 27E13, India.

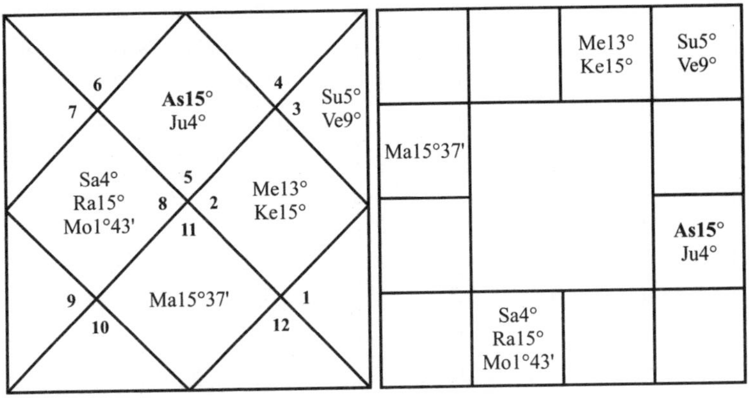

		Me13° Ke15°	Su5° Ve9°
Ma15°37'			
			As15° Ju4°
	Sa4° Ra15° Mo1°43'		

South Indian chart values:
- 6, 7: As15° Ju4°
- 4, 3: Su5° Ve9°
- Sa4° Ra15° Mo1°43', 8, 5, 2: Me13° Ke15°, 11
- 9, 10: Ma15°37', 1, 12

Besides the dhanakaraka, the Sun, Mercury, Venus, Mars and Jupiter become significators for financial prosperity. The Sun is strong and placed in the house of income. The Rahu-Ketu axis, in their signs of debilitation, is close to the most effective points of the fourth and tenth houses and severely damages the houses occupied as well as aspected. The weak Saturn, in its infancy, is severely afflicted by the most malefic planet, the Moon. The weakness and affliction of Saturn damages Mars as Saturn is the dispositor of Mars. The influence of Jupiter is not pronounced as it is far away from the most effective point. Mercury is severely afflicted by the Rahu-Ketu axis.

The operation of the sub-periods of weak, afflicted and afflicting planets did not allow the native to get established financially. The performance of propitiatory remedies for Rahu-Ketu and the Moon and wearing of a Kavach was suggested. This was for strengthening the functional benefic planets, the Sun, Venus, Mercury, Mars, Jupiter and Saturn to bear the influence of the natal/ transit afflictions of the functional malefic planets. The wearing of the Kavach in an auspicious time helped the native in a big way.

Chart 35

Male born 21st October 1957, 1955 Hrs. 91E45 26N11, India.

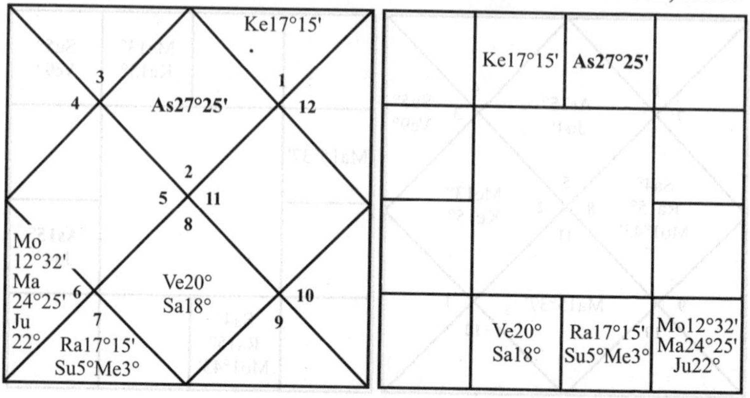
Ke17°15'
3
1
4
As27°25'
12
2
5
11
8
Mo
12°32'
Ma
24°25'
6
Ve20°
Sa18°
10
Ju
22°
7
9
Ra17°15'
Su5°Me3°
Ke17°15'
As27°25'
Ve20°
Sa18°
Ra17°15'
Su5°Me3°
Mo12°32'
Ma24°25'
Ju22°

In this nativity, besides the dhanakaraka, Saturn, the Moon, Jupiter and Mercury become the significators of financial resources. Saturn is strong in this chart. The Sun, being lord of the fourth house, is in its sign of debilitation and it is badly placed in the sixth house ruling debts, disputes and diseases. The weak combust Mercury is also placed in the sixth house. The close influence of the functional malefic Mars on the most effective point of the eleventh house caused losses and obstructions in the sources of income. The close influence of the functional malefic Mars, by way of conjunction with Jupiter, the planet ruling inheritance, caused enormous loss of wealth to the father. The placement of the Moon in the fifth house indicates some gains in life through the entrepreneurial ventures. However, the Moon, as a significator, indicates lots of changes in life and weakness of dispositor of the Moon in this case induced frequent changes in the professional pursuits of this native. The use of the propitiatory astral remedies for the functional malefic planets and use of a Kavach for the weak functional benefic planets in an auspicious time were suggested for improvements in the matter of health and financial resources.

Chapter 6

Handling Psychiatric Problems

With materialism all pervading, everybody is becoming ambitious and trying to compete with others in terms of materialistic possessions. Money has become the master. For earning more and more and acquiring good status in life, professional education is the one simple way. Therefore, people are putting more and more pressure on their children for success in competitive exams. This is causing psychiatric problems to the children when they fail to cope up with the pressures. Another reason is the changing values in the societies as a consequence of globalization. People are finding it difficult to cope with changing behavior patterns and life styles. The established moral values are being ignored. Taking all these together, there are increased and unbearable mental pressures in the emotional relationships, studies, pursuing changing life styles and coping with the competitive activities in education, business and job matters. Therefore, it is not only necessary that an astrologer be able to identify the psychiatric problem, but also handle it with suggestions of astral remedies.

The Significators of the Psychiatric Problems

The Planets	The Moon and Mercury
The Houses	Fourth and fifth
The Signs	Cancer and Leo

The Moon is the significator of mind while Mercury rules the nerves and communicative capabilities controlled by the brain. The fourth house signifies the mental status while the fifth house signifies the power of the brain in receiving, analyzing, absorbing and rejecting the various messages caused by the planetary influences during the sub-periods of various planets. The signs Cancer and Leo are significators of mental potentialities. The Sun ruling the Leo sign rules the organizational power of the person. The organization power helps the person in sorting out the mental confusion and see the things clearly. The significations of the signs fructify through the strength of their lords.

The psychiatric problems can be long-term as well as short-term. The natal afflictions to the significators cause long-term problems. The transit afflictions cause short-term problems. Needless to say, the afflictions are caused by the close conjunctions/ aspects of the functional malefic planets in a nativity to other planets/houses.

By way of a few case studies, we shall see the horoscope analysis for psychiatric problems and the results where the astral remedies were administered.

Chart 36

Male born 15th January 1973, 0055 Hrs.

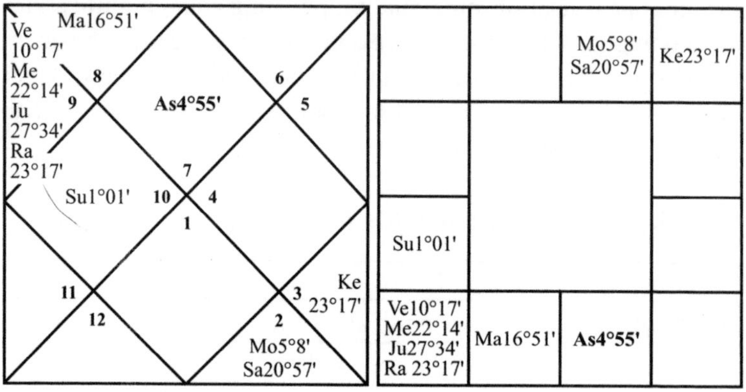

Ve 10°17' Me 22°14' Ju 27°34' Ra 23°17' (8, 9) Ma16°51'	As4°55' (7, 10) Su1°01'	(6, 5)	
(11, 12)		(1, 4)	Ke 23°17' (2, 3) Mo5°8' Sa20°57'

		Mo5°8' Sa20°57'	Ke23°17'
Su1°01'			
Ve10°17' Me22°14' Ju27°34' Ra 23°17'	Ma16°51'	As4°55'	

Mercury, Rahu and Ketu are the functional malefic planets in this nativity. Rahu closely afflicts Mercury and Jupiter. Saturn, being lord of the fifth house, along with the Moon, is badly placed in the eighth house and both of these planets have been rendered weak. The significator planets, the Moon and Mercury, are both weak, and the Moon is badly afflicted. The Sun is in the state of infancy. Because of the natal afflictions, the psychiatric problems manifested in this case for a very long duration. The native was a student of engineering when suddenly during the sub-period of the Moon in the main period of Mars mental stress increased. Because of the weakness of the Moon due to bad placement, the native could not cope up with mental stress and started complaining of headache, body pain and sleeplessness. In the following sub-period of Rahu in its own main period, the situation became so grim that the native could not return to studies. Finally, the large gap compelled the discontinuance of studies. The medical treatment could not help the person. In February 1994, the native's parents approached for astrological remedies. The native was prescribed wearing of a Kavach and performance of charities for Mercury, Rahu and Ketu. The performance of the astral remedies could bring the native out of the difficult situation and from the year 1995 when the sub-period of Jupiter was in progress the native started visiting the family business place. The native fully recovered from his psychiatric problem and started handling a family business unit independently. The wearing of the Kavach continues to provide strength to the weak planets like Saturn, the Moon, the Sun and Jupiter in the nativity.

Chart 37

Male born 25th March 1981, 1728 Hrs. New Delhi, India.

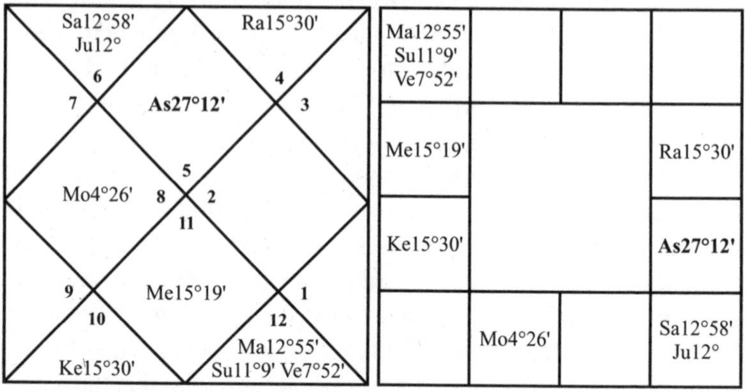
Sa12°58'
Ju12°
Ra15°30'
6
4
7
As27°12'
3
5
Mo4°26'
8
2
11
9
Me15°19'
1
10
12
Ma12°55'
Ke15°30'
Su11°9' Ve7°52'
Ma12°55'
Su11°9'
Ve7°52'
Me15°19'
Ra15°30'
Ke15°30'
As27°12'
Mo4°26'
Sa12°58'
Ju12°

The Moon is in its sign of debilitation. The fifth lord, Jupiter, along with Saturn, is under the close aspect of Ketu from the sixth house. The badly placed Sun and Mars are under the close aspect of Rahu from the twelfth house. Although Mercury is apparently well placed and unafflicted, the sub-period of Mercury was of little help due to the affliction of its dispositor. As soon as the sub-period of Mars in the main period of Saturn started there were problems to the father in his business and from the Government. The circumstances at home created tension for the native. The onset of the sub-period of Rahu in the main period of Saturn and the affliction of the Sun by Rahu triggered acute tension for the native that involved his father as well, as the Sun is significator of father. In August 1994, the astral remedies were sought when the natal afflictions and the long duration were explained to the father. Though the astral remedies were started but to cut short the duration, more stress was placed by the father of the native on the psychiatric treatment in comparison to the astral remedies. The prolonged psychiatric treatment proved to be of no help and the native's father returned to astral remedies. The performance of astral remedies helped in steering the native clear of the problem. The child started leading a comparatively better life and started participating in the family business. The problem, however, took the toll on studies.

Chart 38

Female born in May 1975.

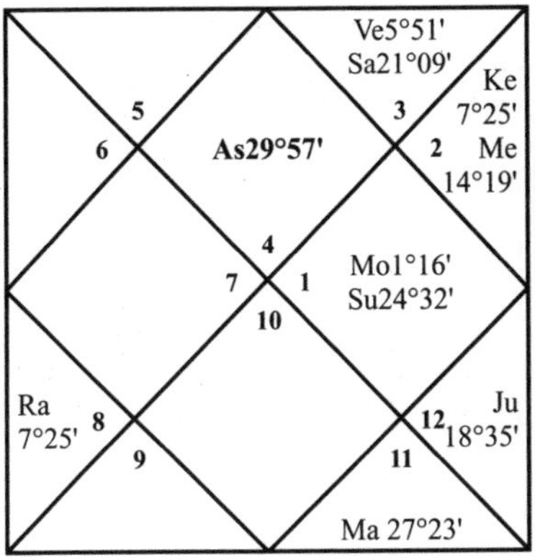

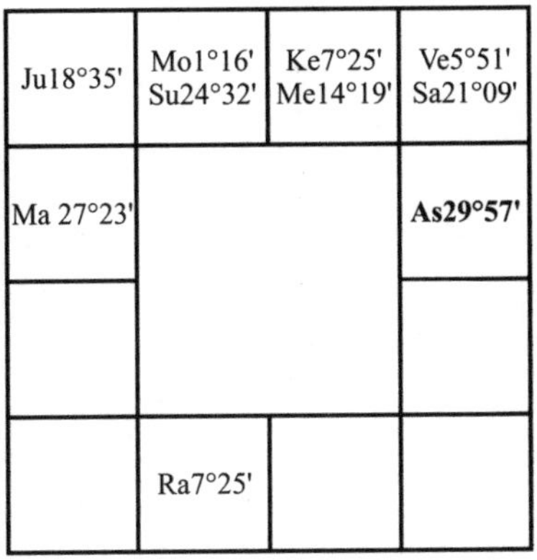

	Ve5°51' Sa21°09' Ke 7°25' Me 14°19'		
5 / 6 As29°57' / 3 / 2 4 / 7 / 1 / 10 Mo1°16' Su24°32' Ra 7°25' / 8 / 9 / 12 / 11 / Ju18°35' Ma 27°23'			

	Ju18°35'	Mo1°16' Su24°32'	Ke7°25' Me14°19'	Ve5°51' Sa21°09'
Ma 27°23'				As29°57'
Ra7°25'				

The lord of the fourth house, Venus, is badly placed. There is no mooltrikona sign in the fifth house, and as such the lord of the fifth house is not under consideration. Mercury is strong. The Moon is weak due to infancy and badly placed dispositor. The lord of the sign Leo, the Sun, is well placed but weak due to weak dispositor. The chart does not indicate long term problems as there are no natal afflictions. The natal Mercury came under the close aspect of the most malefic planet, Saturn, from June, 1996. Simultaneously, transit Rahu also afflicted natal Mercury in July and August, 1996 The continued stress for over three months necessitated consultation with a psychiatrist. The lack of improvement compelled the parents of the native to seek astral remedies which helped the native with immediate improvement during the later part of November 1996. The affliction of natal Rahu to transit Saturn and the transit conjunction of Saturn and Ketu in later part of December 1996 gave rise to another disturbance. As there is no natal affliction, the native was advised that the performance of astral remedies on continued basis would arrest the recurrence of such a problem in future.

Chart 39

Male born 15th April 1978, 1230 Hrs. Guwahati, India.

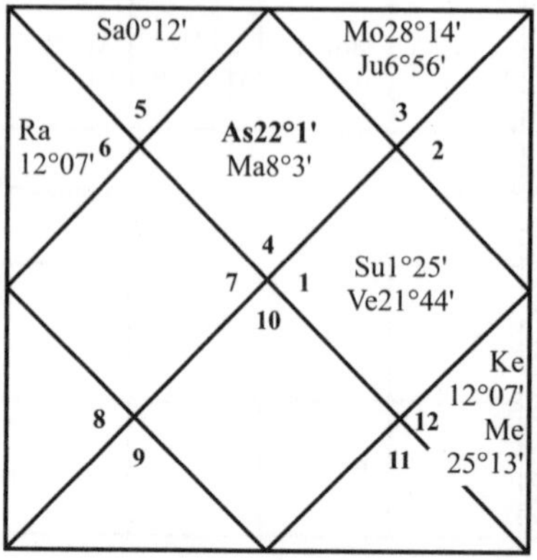

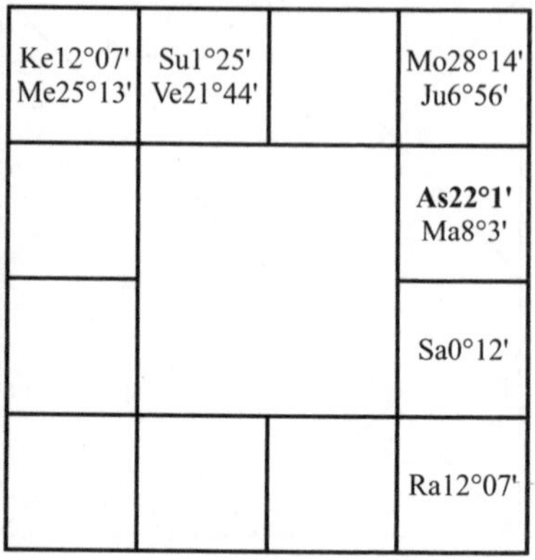

Sa0°12'			

Left diamond chart:
- 5: Sa0°12'
- 6: Ra 12°07'
- 3: Mo28°14' Ju6°56'
- 2
- As22°1' Ma8°3'
- 4
- 7
- 1
- 10
- Su1°25' Ve21°44'
- 8
- 9
- 12: Ke 12°07' Me 25°13'
- 11

Right square chart:

Ke12°07' Me25°13'	Su1°25' Ve21°44'		Mo28°14' Ju6°56'
			As22°1' Ma8°3'
			Sa0°12'
			Ra12°07'

The Moon and Mercury are weak. The Moon is badly placed and in old age while Mercury is combust and debilitated. The lord of the fourth house is well placed and unafflicted but weak due to debilitation and affliction of its dispositor, Mars. There is no mooltrikona sign in the fifth house. Besides being weakly disposed, the Sun is also in the state of infancy. The chart does show some natal weaknesses. During the sub-period of the Moon, due to the natal afflictions and weaknesses the native suffered from psychic problem and had to undergo psychiatric treatment. The school was discontinued. The problem showed its acute stage when the transit Rahu exerted its stationary influence over the natal Rahu between August 96 and November 96. The astral remedies were sought towards the end of November 1996, which helped. Use of Kavach for strengthening the weak, badly placed and afflicted functional benefic planets and propitiatory measures were suggested for the functional malefic planets, Rahu, Ketu, Saturn and Jupiter. The performance of the astral remedies helped and the native is pursuing his studies in a normal way.

Chart 40

Female born in December 1972.

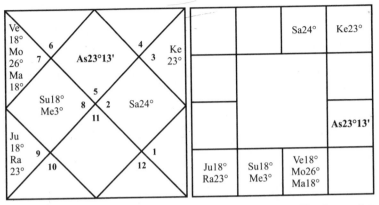

Rahu exerts its exact influence over the most effective point of the fifth house. Ketu exerts its close influence over the Moon by way of fifth aspect. There is no mooltrikona sign in the fourth house. The fifth house lord is placed in the fifth house but the affliction of Rahu/Ketu axis on the most effective point of the fifth house takes precedence over the good placement of Jupiter. The lord of the fifth house turns weak as it is placed in an afflicted house. The Sun is weak as its mooltrikona sign is afflicted. Though Mercury is well placed, it is weak due to infancy. The sub-period of afflicting Rahu was in operation from May 1995 to March 1998. Due to the exact affliction of Rahu, life was fully disturbed on the marital front. The prolonged stationary influence of Rahu on the most effective point of the second house between April 96 and May 96, resulted in separation from the in-laws family and the native suffered from psychiatric problem and had to undergo treatment. Neither the native was in a position to perform propitiatory remedies nor was she ready to wear the Kavach due to acute affliction of Rahu. Whenever Rahu closely afflicts the fifth house, the improvement becomes very difficult and people start suspecting that the person is under the influence of evil spirits or some black magic activity is perceived. The direction of treatment both medical and astral thus gets lost resulting in many more problems to the native. The performance of astral remedies by the parents of the native in such cases bring slow improvement which can be accelerated if the native himself/herself performs the astral remedies.

Chart 41

Male born 31st January 1975, 1730 Hrs. 78E27 17N26, India.

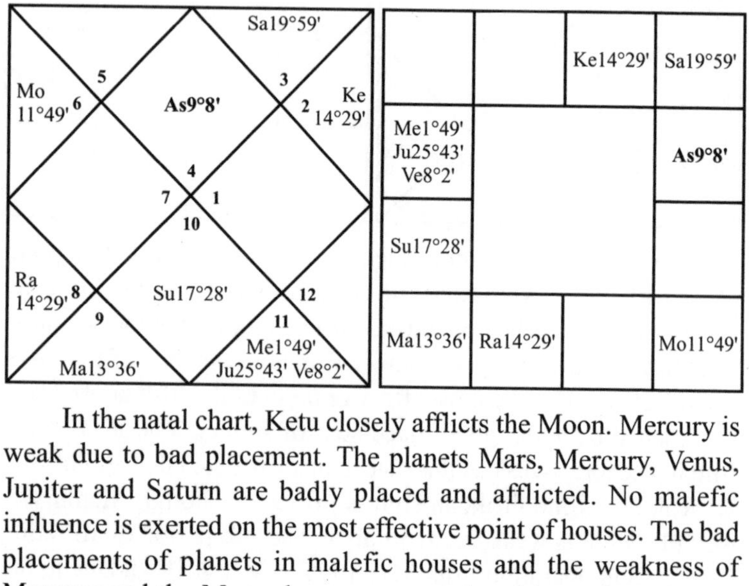

In the natal chart, Ketu closely afflicts the Moon. Mercury is weak due to bad placement. The planets Mars, Mercury, Venus, Jupiter and Saturn are badly placed and afflicted. No malefic influence is exerted on the most effective point of houses. The bad placements of planets in malefic houses and the weakness of Mercury and the Moon, however, caused problems from time to time due to transit influences as also in the sub-periods of the concerned planets. When the transits of the most malefic planet, Saturn, and the Rahu/Ketu axis exerted their simultaneous influence on the natal Moon, the boy suffered from mental disturbance due to obstructions in concentration. The boy was under psychiatric treatment in January 1997. When there was no improvement, alternate therapies were sought thinking that the boy is under the influence of some evil spirits. When it was brought to our notice, it was advised that there was no impact of evil spirits and that there was no psychiatric problem, either. It was told to them that the boy will be all right by the end of February 1997, when the transit impact of Saturn began to separate. Early improvement was indicated with the help of propitiatory remedies for Saturn, Rahu and Ketu , which did help, and the boy resumed his studies towards the end of February 1997.

Chapter 7

Cutting Down Delay in Marriage

Marriage is one of the important aspects of life. Delay in marriage brings with it many problems and depression. When all the worldly requirements for the marriage exist and the efforts fail, people come and take astral help. The divine science of astrology has the twin capability of identifying the reasons for the delay and of applying astral remedies to expedite the marriage by cutting down the delay. Let us discuss both these aspects.

Marriage Significators

1) The lord of the seventh house containing a mooltrikona sign is the prime determinant of marriage. In case there is no mooltrikona sign in the seventh house, then the lord of the next mooltrikona sign house signifying marriage (the second, fourth, eighth or twelfth house) becomes the prime determinant. For each ascendant, the prime determinant of marriage is:-

Aries	Venus
Taurus	The Sun
Gemini	Jupiter
Cancer	The Sun
Leo	Saturn
Virgo	Venus
Libra	Mars
Scorpio	Jupiter

Sagittarius	The Moon
Capricorn	The Moon
Aquarius	The Sun
Pisces	Mercury

2)   Venus and Jupiter are significators of marriage for males and females, respectively.

3)   Marriage can also take place: in the sub-periods of the lords of the remaining mooltrikona sign houses signifying marriage; and in the sub-periods of the strong planets placed in the houses signifying marriage. These planets become secondary determinants or significators of marriage.

4)   If the navamsa ascendant contains a mooltrikona sign, then its lord becomes the additional prime determinant for marriage.

If the prime determinant of marriage and the general significator of marriage are strong or fairly strong and there is no affliction to the most effective points of the houses signifying marriage, the marriage takes place at the appropriate time. The good strength of Venus hastens the process. The delay is caused by:

1)   The most effective points of the seventh, fourth and/or second houses being afflicted;

2)   The prime determinant of marriage and/or the secondary determinants being afflicted and/or weak for other reasons.

3)   The general significator of marriage being afflicted and/or weak for other reasons.

4)   The lord of the fourth house being utterly weak.

5)   The lords of the eighth and/or twelfth houses containing a mooltrikona sign being afflicted and/or weak for other reasons.

6)   Whenever the severe affliction involves the seventh house in the case of male natives they lack confidence in their physical power and delay the decision of marriage.

The influence of the functional malefic planets delays while the influence of the most malefic planet delays inordinately and/or denies. The inauspicious influence of the most malefic planet cannot be mellowed without persistent performance of the appropriate astral remedies.

Now, with the help of a few case studies we will discuss the matter for a good grasp of planetary influences causing delay in marriage and application of astral remedies for expediting the marriage:

Chart 42

Female born 11th January 1967, 2200 Hrs. 76E38 28N57, India.

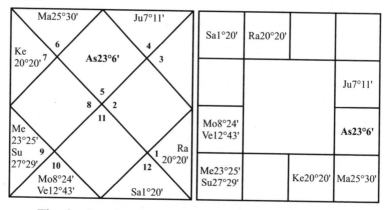

The sign Leo rises in the ascendant. Saturn, becomes the prime determinant of marriage for Leos. Saturn is weak in the chart due to infancy and bad placement. Venus being navamsa ascendant lord becomes the additional prime determinant of marriage. Venus is weak as it is badly placed. All the secondary determinants of marriage, Mercury, the Moon and Mars are weak. Mercury is weak due to combustion, close affliction of Rahu and weak dispositor. The Moon is weak due to combustion and bad placement. Mars is weak due to the weakness of dispositor, Mercury. Jupiter, being also the general significator of husband, is weak due to bad placement and the weakness of the dispositor, the Moon. Besides being weak for other reasons, Jupiter is closely afflicted by the most malefic planet, and Mercury is closely afflicted by Rahu. The most effective point of the seventh house is closely aspected and afflicted by the functional malefic planet, Ketu. The afflictions and other weaknesses in the chart were delaying the finalization of marriage when the help of astrology was sought. The propitiatory astral remedies for Rahu, Ketu and the Moon were suggested besides wearing a Kavach containing the mystical numbers of the Sun, Mercury, Jupiter, Venus, Saturn and Mars. The performance of astral remedies helped in solemnization of the marriage in early 1995 during the sub-period of Mercury in the main period of Rahu which was in progress since 9th October, 1992. But for the remedies, the weak Saturn, the afflicted Mercury and the afflicted badly placed Jupiter may not have blessed the native with the marriage.

Chart 43

Female born 21st August 1953, 0420 Hrs. 88E23 22N35, India.

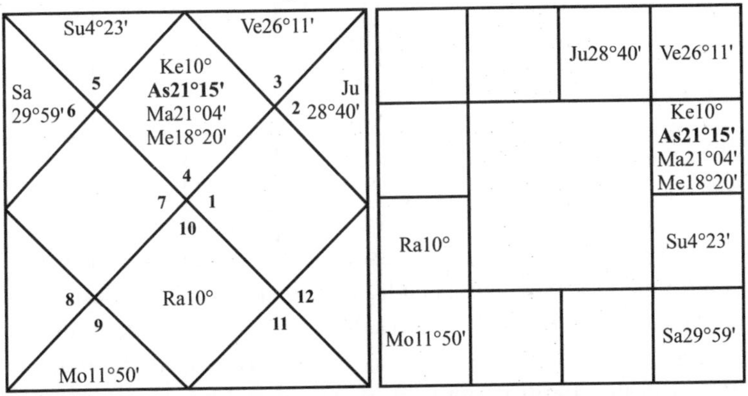
Su4°23'
Ve26°11'
Ke10°
As21°15'
Ma21°04'
Me18°20'
Sa 29°59'
Ju 28°40'
5
3
6
2
4
7
1
10
Ra10°
8
12
9
11
Mo11°50'
Ju28°40'
Ve26°11'
Ke10°
As21°15'
Ma21°04'
Me18°20'
Ra10°
Su4°23'
Mo11°50'
Sa29°59'

The sign Cancer rises in the ascendant. The Sun becomes the prime determinant of marriage in this chart. The Sun is in the second house and is fairly strong. There is no mooltrikona sign in navamsa ascendant. The lord of the fourth house, Venus, is badly placed and has become weak. Venus is closely afflicted by the aspect of the most malefic planet, Saturn. The lord of the house of marital ties,

Saturn, is very weak as it is in the thirtieth degree. This weak Saturn is also closely afflicted by the functional malefic Jupiter.

In this case, the lord of the fourth house is under the severe affliction of the most malefic planet and hence it caused a lot of delay in the marriage. The propitiatory astral remedies suggested for Saturn, Jupiter, Rahu and Ketu helped in marriage during the sub-period of Saturn in the main period of the Moon. Later on, for prosperity and good health, the native also took advantage of the Kavach for the functional benefic planets, the Moon, the Sun, Venus, Mercury and Mars.

Chart 44

Female born 17th March 1967, 1707 Hrs. 77E13 28N39, India.

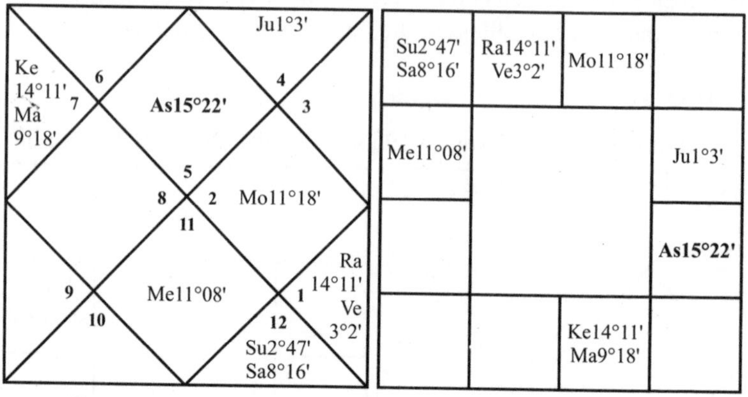

North Indian chart:
- As15°22', Ju1°3'
- Ke 14°11', Ma 9°18' (house 7, 6)
- Mo11°18'
- Me11°08'
- Ra 14°11', Ve 3°2', Su2°47', Sa8°16'
- Houses numbered: 6, 4, 3, 7, 5, 8, 2, 11, 9, 10, 12, 1

South Indian chart:

Su2°47' Sa8°16'	Ra14°11' Ve3°2'	Mo11°18'	
Me11°08'			Ju1°3'
			As15°22'
	Ke14°11' Ma9°18'		

The sign, Leo, rises in the ascendant. Saturn, being the prime determinant of marriage, is badly placed and combust. Sun being navamsa ascendant lord becomes the additional prime determinant of marriage. The Sun is weak as it is badly placed. Mercury is placed in the mooltrikona sign of Saturn and has become weak. The Moon is the most malefic planet and its close aspect on the most effective point of the fourth house is undesirable for the purpose of marriage. The most effective point of the seventh house is closely afflicted by the aspect of Ketu besides the seventh lord being combust and badly placed. The general significator of marriage, Jupiter, is in infancy and is very weak as the most effective point of its mooltrikona sign is closely afflicted by Rahu. **The extreme weakness of Jupiter also robs the person of discipline in life, which is required for strict performance of the astral remedies to ward off the affliction of the most malefic planet. The native's mother sought astrological help in the year 1995. The astral remedies were prescribed but the native never performed them with sincerity and regularity. The result is that she remained unmarried.**

Chart 45

Male born 30th June 1965, 0200 Hrs. 77E42 29N00, India.

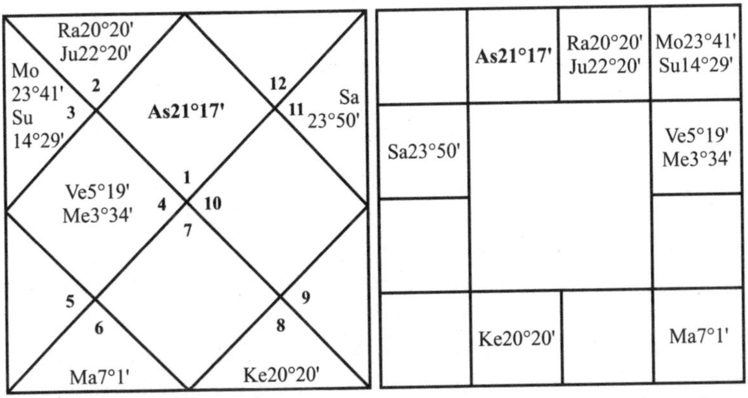

	As21°17'	Ra20°20' Ju22°20'	Mo23°41' Su14°29'
Sa23°50'			Ve5°19' Me3°34'
Ke20°20'			Ma7°1'

Chart (North Indian style, left):
- Ra20°20' Ju22°20', Mo 23°41', Su 14°29' (house 2, 3)
- As21°17' (house 12, 11)
- Sa 23°50'
- Ve5°19' Me3°34'
- Ma7°1'
- Ke20°20'

The sign Aries rises in the ascendant. Venus is the prime determinant of marriage as well as the general significator for wife. Venus being navamsa ascendant lord becomes the additional prime determinant of marriage. Venus is weak as it is closely afflicted by the functional malefic planet, Mercury. The most effective points of the second, fourth, eighth and twelfth houses are under the close affliction of Rahu and/or Ketu. Jupiter, a secondary determinant of marriage for being placed in the second house, is also closely afflicted by the Rahu/Ketu axis. Due to severe afflictions, the marriage of the native was inordinately delayed in spite of being a professionally settled medico. The native asked for astral help in March 1995, when he was under the sub-period of Jupiter in the main period of Saturn. The application of propitiatory remedies for Mercury, Rahu and Ketu and use of Kavach for functional benefic planets helped the native and his marriage was solemnized in the end of the year 1995.

Chart 46

Male born 28th September 1947, 0050 Hrs. 75E22 28N22, India.

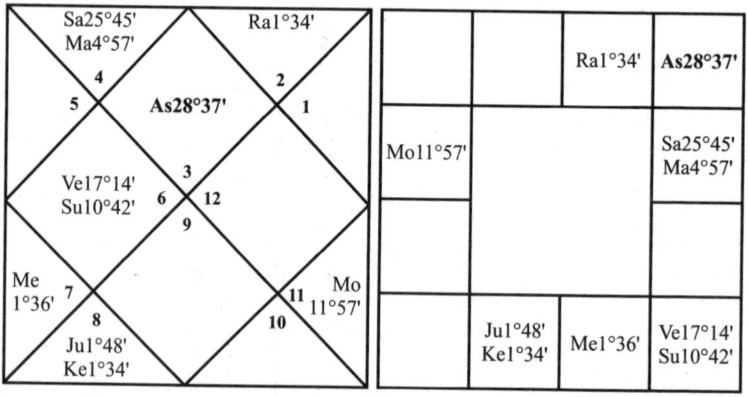
Sa25°45'
Ma4°57'
Ra1°34'
4
2
5
As28°37'
1
3
Ve17°14'
Su10°42'
6
12
9
Me
1°36'
7
11
Mo
11°57'
8
10
Ju1°48'
Ke1°34'
Ra1°34'
As28°37'
Mo11°57'
Sa25°45'
Ma4°57'
Ju1°48'
Ke1°34'
Me1°36'
Ve17°14'
Su10°42'

The prime determinant of marriage, Jupiter, is in infancy, badly placed, and exactly conjunct with the most malefic planet, Ketu. The general significator for wife, Venus, is weak as it is combust, debilitated and its dispositor is weak. The lord of the fourth house, Mercury, is weak due to infancy and the weakness of its dispositor. There is no mooltrikona sign in navamsa ascendant. The marriage of the person was inordinately delayed despite the native being professionally qualified and suitably employed. **The single degree or exact affliction of the most malefic planet always causes inordinate delay or denial. When the planet under the exact degree affliction is also weak for other reasons, it makes the person vulnerable to prolonged or cancerous illness on health front. Whenever the severe affliction involves the seventh house in the case of male natives they lack confidence in their physical power and delay the decision of marriage.** The native suffered from the malfunctioning of kidneys. The marriage of the native was inordinately delayed. The native married in 48th year. The marriage was not a happy affair from the very beginning. Astral remedies were prescribed for the continuance of marriage and for protection of health problems.

Chart 47

Male born 5th November 1940, 0615 Hrs. 88E23 22N35, India.

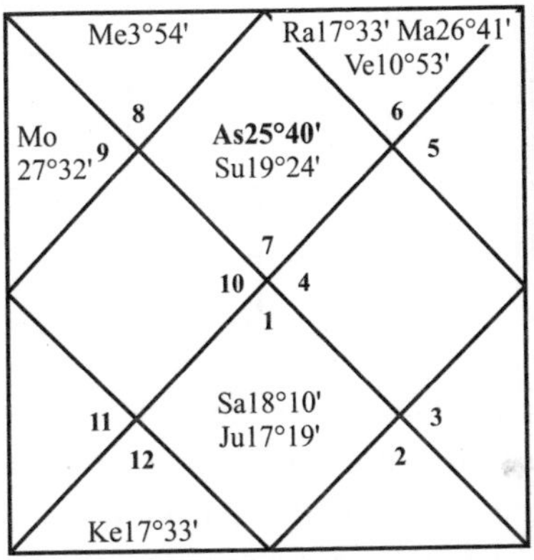
Me3°54'
Ra17°33' Ma26°41'
Ve10°53'
8
6
Mo
27°32'
9
As25°40'
Su19°24'
5
7
10
4
1
Sa18°10'
Ju17°19'
11
3
12
2
Ke17°33'

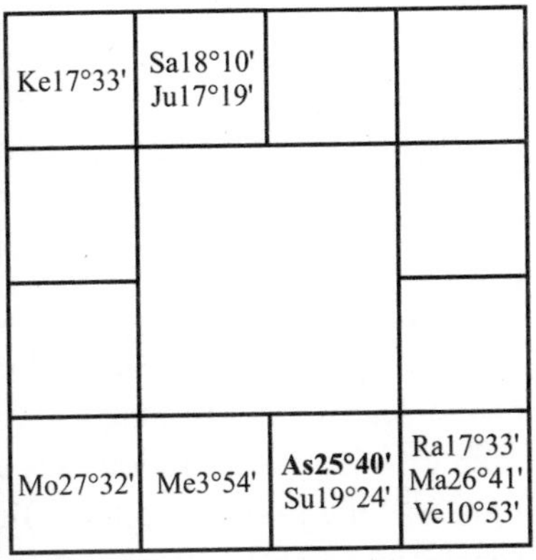
Ke17°33'
Sa18°10'
Ju17°19'
Mo27°32'
Me3°54'
As25°40'
Su19°24'
Ra17°33'
Ma26°41'
Ve10°53'

Mars becomes the prime determinant of marriage. Mars is weak as it is badly placed and in old age. The significator for wife, Venus, is badly placed, debilitated and is weak. There is no mooltrikona sign in navamsa ascendant. Saturn and Jupiter, placed in the seventh house, become weak due to the weakness of their dispositor, Mars. Saturn is debilitated, as well. Due to the weakness of all planets indicating marriage, the marriage of the native was inordinately delayed. The native suddenly went in for marriage at the age of 56 years and continuously suffered from nervous weakness, stiff neck and sciatica pain.

Chart 48

Male born 16th September 1965, 2202 Hrs. 80E40 16N34, India.

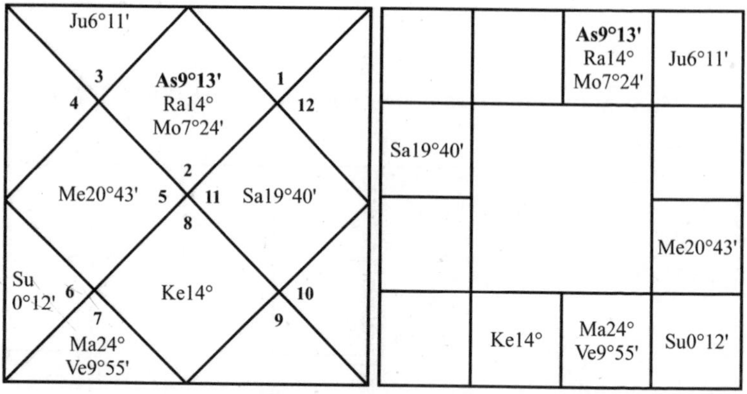
Ju6°11'
3
4
As9°13'
Ra14°
Mo7°24'
1
12
2
Me20°43'
5
11
Sa19°40'
8
Su
0°12'
6
Ke14°
10
7
9
Ma24°
Ve9°55'
As9°13'
Ra14°
Mo7°24'
Ju6°11'
Sa19°40'
Me20°43'
Ke14°
Ma24°
Ve9°55'
Su0°12'

The sign Taurus rises in the ascendant. The Sun becomes the prime determinant of marriage. The Sun lacks power due to utter infancy. There is no mooltrikona sign in navamsa ascendant. The most malefic planet, Jupiter, afflicts the most effective point of the second and eighth houses, and the general significator of marriage, Venus. Afflicted Venus exactly afflicts the most effective point of the twelfth house. The weakness of the Sun and the afflictions caused by Jupiter and Venus delayed marriage inordinately. Jupiter in this chart becomes a significator of marriage due to placement near the most effective point of the second house. But its role as most malefic planet takes precedence over the former role. **The close affliction of the most malefic planet over the most effective points of the second and/or fourth houses severely obstructs the formation of the family and denies continuity of family without the astral remedies.** As Jupiter is the most malefic planet and as it is involved in close afflictions in the natal chart, the native is not regular in the sincere performance of astral remedies and hence the delay in marriage continues.

Chart 49

Male born 18th October 1953, 1830 Hrs. 71W38 42N34 TZ 5.00 Hrs.

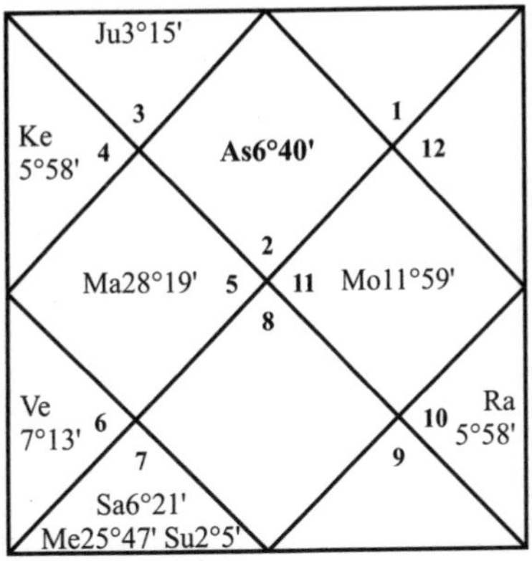

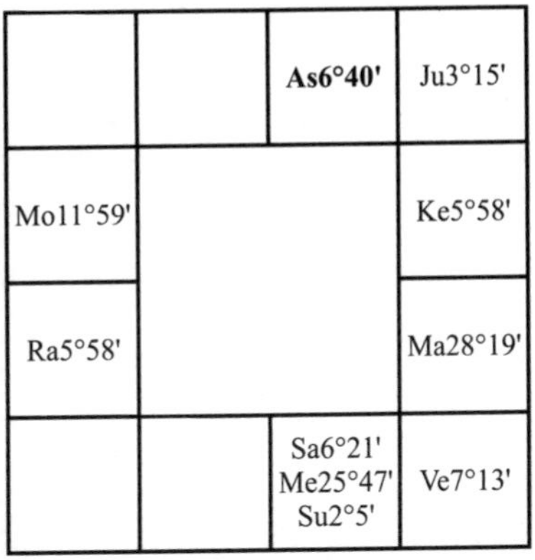

Ju3°15'			
Ke 5°58' (4)	(3) As6°40' (1) (2) (12)		
Ma28°19' (5) (8)	(11) Mo11°59'		
Ve 7°13' (6) (7)	(9) (10) Ra 5°58'		
Sa6°21' Me25°47' Su2°5'			

		As6°40'	Ju3°15'
Mo11°59'			Ke5°58'
Ra5°58'			Ma28°19'
		Sa6°21' Me25°47' Su2°5'	Ve7°13'

Taurus rises in the ascendant. The prime determinant of marriage, the Sun, is extremely weak as it is badly placed, in infancy and is debilitated in rasi and navamsa. The Sun is also closely afflicted by the most malefic planet, Jupiter. The general significator of marriage, Venus, is very weak as it is debilitated, placed in an afflicted house and is closely afflicted by Rahu. Saturn being navamsa ascendant lord becomes the additional prime determinant of marriage. Saturn is weak as it is badly placed, combust and closely afflicted. The most malefic planet, Jupiter, also afflicts the most effective point of the second and eighth houses in the main chart. The most effective point of the seventh house is severely afflicted by the exact aspect of Ketu. The marriage was inordinately delayed. The native was married in the year 1990. The native sought astral remedies for progeny in the year 1995, as he was not still blessed with a child. The most effective points of the fifth and second houses are afflicted and the primary and secondary significators for progeny, Mercury, Jupiter and the Sun, are all weak.

Chart 50

Female born 5th November 1965, 1625 Hrs. 77E13 28N39, India.

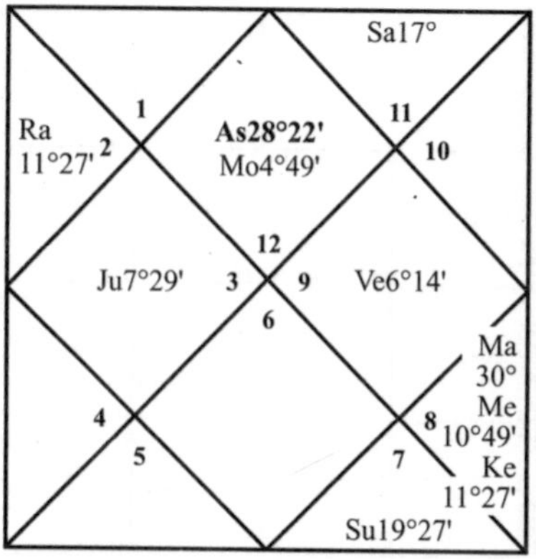
Sa17°
1
11
Ra 11°27'
2
As28°22'
Mo4°49'
10
12
Ju7°29'
3
9
Ve6°14'
6
Ma 30°
Me 10°49'
4
8
Ke 11°27'
5
7
Su19°27'

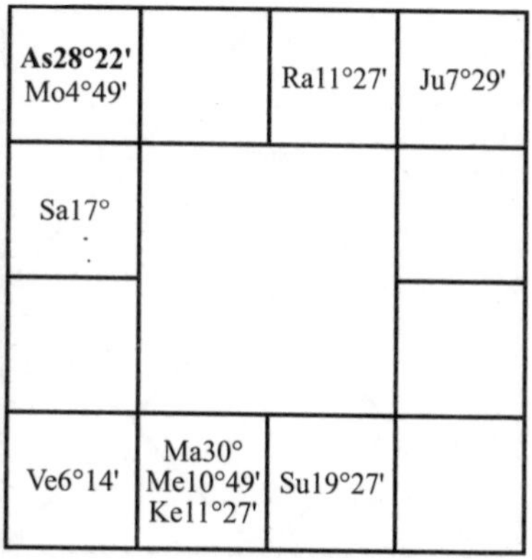
As28°22'
Mo4°49'
Ra11°27'
Ju7°29'
Sa17°
Ve6°14'
Ma30°
Me10°49'
Ke11°27'
Su19°27'

The prime determinant of marriage, Mercury, is in exact conjunction with Ketu. The lord of the house of family, Mars, is in the thirtieth degree and hence very weak. The significator for husband, Jupiter, is closely afflicted by the most malefic planet. Due to these inauspicious planetary influences, the efforts of the parents for finalizing marriage of this girl were not successful. Astrological help was sought in the year 1990, when the native was running the sub-period of the Moon in the main period of Mercury. The native was not prepared for performance of the astral remedies which is quite clear from the affliction of Jupiter by most malefic planet, Venus. The native thought that as she belongs to a well-established and respectable family, is well educated and beautiful, the marriage will take place within the next four to six months. Seeing the weakness of the next sub-period lord, Mars, and the following sub-period of severely afflicting Rahu, it was indicated that the marriage may not take place for the next 2 or 3 years if the astral remedies were not performed. The girl was adamant. As the luck would have it, the marriage could not be finalized for the next two years. Again the parents asked for astrological help and confirmed that the girl was ready to perform the astral remedies as prescribed. With the help of the astral remedies, the marriage took place in December 1992. The lord of the fifth house is faily strong and placed in the ascendant which blessed the native with a Master's degree.

Chart 51

Female born 9th February 1966, 1323 Hrs. 77E13 28N39, India.

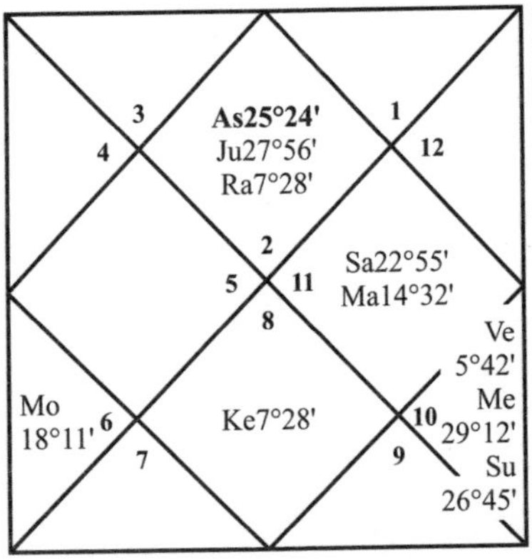

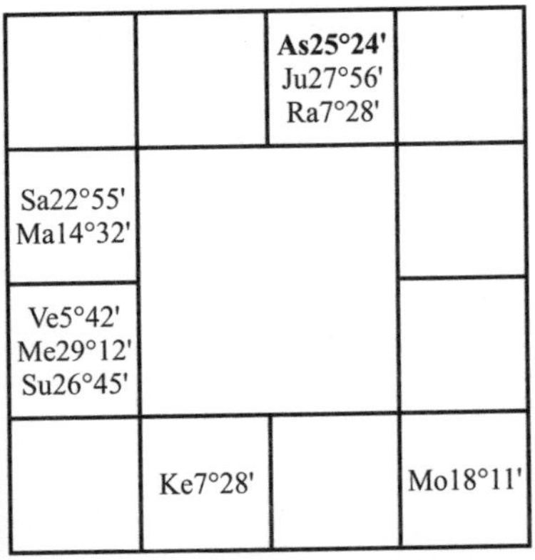

The sign Taurus rises in the ascendant. The primary significator of marriage, the Sun, is closely afflicted by Jupiter, the most malefic planet. Jupiter also afflicts the most effective point of the seventh house. The Sun being navamsa ascendant lord becomes the additional prime determinant of marriage, as well. The Sun is weak due to strong affliction, as earlier indicated. The delay in marriage was indicated. In such cases, marriage cannot be finalized without the performance of appropriate astral remedies. The position of Jupiter as a significator of marriage is weak as it is in the 28th degree. As luck would have it, the native was not ready to perform the astral remedies. The marriage could not be finalized even in a period of more than two years in spite of the persistent efforts of the parents. The native agreed to perform the astral remedies only in August 1991, when it was indicated that the marriage may be finalized before March 1992. The marriage of the native took place in January, 1992.

The natives are advised to continue the performance of astral remedies even after the marriage for enjoying a peaceful and harmonious married life. The affliction of the most malefic planet is as powerful as the feet of 'Angada' in the court of the King Ravana. Only the impact of astral remedies can cut the delay otherwise it denies the marital happiness.

It is hoped that the case studies will help the readers in comprehending the techniques of locating delay in marriage and application of astral remedies, accordingly.

Chapter 8

Identifying Early Widowhood

In this Chapter, we are taking up the case studies on the death of husband in the early years of marriage. All these cases on death of the husband were brought up for astral analysis after the tragic happening had taken place. We are quite confident that the simple preventive astral remedies discussed earlier are even helpful in such cases for prolonging the life and save one from the tragic happenings in life. The basis of this belief is that the strong indications of cancerous disease in various nativities were prevented with the help of the preventive astral remedies. The loss of husband is shown by the affliction(s) to one or more of the following weak planets/houses:-

- The houses signifying marriage and their lords.

- Jupiter as significator for the husband.

- Venus as significator for marriage.

- The sign Libra, which is the seventh house of the natural zodiac.

Amongst the functional malefic planets under the Systems' Approach as brought out and detailed here, and in the book "Systems' Approach for Interpreting Horoscopes", the lord of the sixth house, Ketu, the lord of the twelfth house and the lord of the eighth house show malefic impact in the ascending order. That is why the title of "most malefic planet' has been given to the lord of the eighth house containing a mooltrikona sign. This title passes on to others if no mooltrikona sign is placed in the eighth house.

The death takes place in the sub-periods of significators of marriage that are afflicted and/or weak for other reasons. The houses signifying marriage and the primary, secondary and general significators of marriage have been brought out in the previous chapter. **This aspect of identifying early widowhood is important while doing match mating and analyzing the chart of a would be bride.** In this background, we will take up the case studies for better understanding of the subject.

Chart 52

Female born 15th June 1962, 2000Hrs. 81E51 25N27, India.

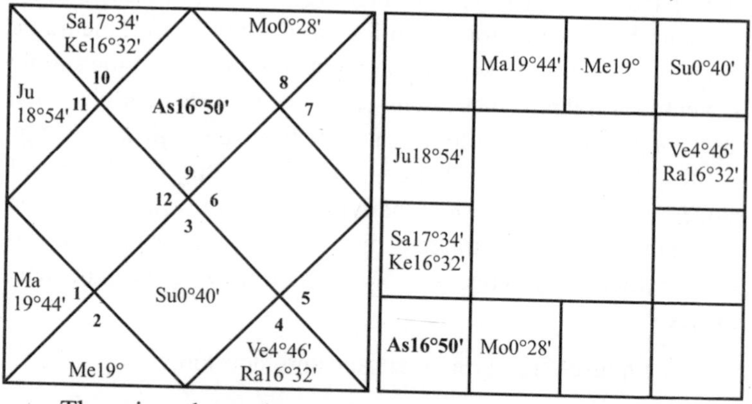

	Ma19°44'	Me19°	Su0°40'
Ju18°54'			Ve4°46' Ra16°32'
Sa17°34' Ke16°32'			
As16°50'	Mo0°28'		

The prime determinant of marriage, the Moon, is very weak as it is badly placed, debilitated, in infancy and the most effective points of its mooltrikona sign house and its house of placement are exactly afflicted by the Rahu/Ketu axis and by Rahu, respectively. The significator of marriage, Venus, is also very weak as it is placed in the severely afflicted eighth house and its dispositor is very weak. Rahu-Ketu axis closely afflicts the most effective points of the second, fourth, eighth and twelfth houses pertaining to marital affairs. Ketu is closely conjunct with Saturn, the dispositor of the general significator of husband, Jupiter, weakening both Saturn and Jupiter. The weakness of all the significators of marriage and the exact affliction to the most effective points of the houses pertaining to marital affairs indicated curtailment in the longevity of married life. The native lost her husband at the age of 34 years, in the sub-period of Rahu, conjunct with the most effective point of the eighth house, and in the main period of Mercury. **The results of functional malefic planets become more intense when they are in the malefic houses.**

Chart 53

Female born 17th November 1960, 0930 Hrs. 77E13 28N39, India.

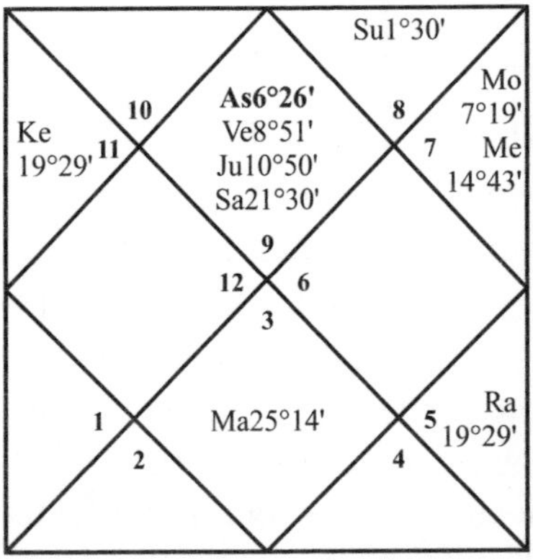

			Ma25°14'
Ke19°29'			
			Ra19°29'
As6°26' Ve8°51' Ju10°50' Sa21°30'	Su1°30'	Mo7°19' Me14°43'	

The prime determinant of marriage in this case is the Moon, which is placed on the most effective point of the eleventh house and is exactly afflicting both the eleventh and the fifth houses indicating serious emotional setback in life. The significator of marriage, Venus, is weak as the most effective point of its mooltrikona sign house is exactly afflicted by the most malefic planet, the Moon. **Whenever a planet becomes a functional malefic planet and is involved in any affliction, its afflicting role takes the precedence over its other roles.** Venus closely influences the most effective point of the ascendant and the seventh house. Venus carries with it the impact of the most malefic planet, the Moon. The most malefic planet exactly afflicts the most effective point of the sign Libra in this nativity. The husband died in the sub-period of the most malefic planet, the Moon, at the age of 29 years.

Chart 54

Female born 30th November 1959, 0225 Hrs. 77E13 28N39, India.

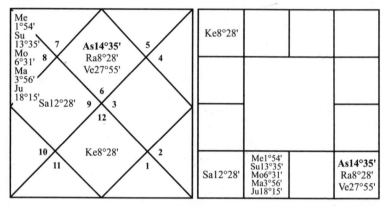

The lord of the second house, ruling family, is debilitated in the birth chart and navamsa, is in old age, and is weak due to the weakness of dispositor. The lord of the sixth house is closely conjunct with the most effective point of the fourth house and afflicts the same. The lord of the fourth house, which is significator for the husband, too, is placed in the third house and is combust and closely afflicted. The lord of the eighth house is closely afflicted by Ketu and is closely afflicting the weak lord of the ascendant. The Sun ruling the house of losses closely afflicts the most effective points of the third and the ninth houses indicating severe setbacks to the fortune of the native. These are indicative of domestic peace suffering on account of inharmonious relationship, health problems to the spouse and accidents. The weakness of the planets representing married life indicates the short duration of married life. The husband died in an accident in the main period of Ketu and the sub-period of Saturn at the age of 37 years.

Chart 55

Female born 28th April 1960, 0600 Hrs. 77E13 28N39, India.

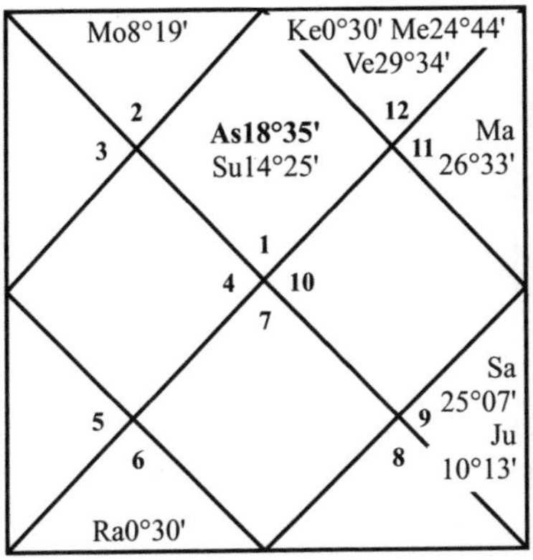
Mo8°19'
Ke0°30' Me24°44'
Ve29°34'
As18°35'
Su14°25'
Ma
26°33'
Sa
25°07'
Ju
10°13'
Ra0°30'
1
2
3
4
5
6
7
8
9
10
11
12

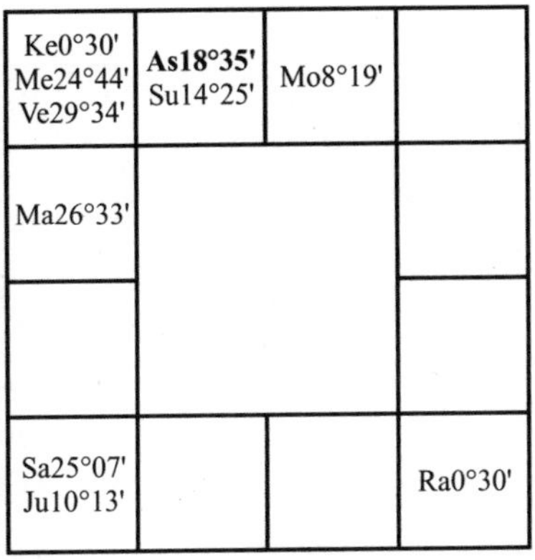
Ke0°30'
Me24°44'
Ve29°34'
As18°35'
Su14°25'
Mo8°19'
Ma26°33'
Sa25°07'
Ju10°13'
Ra0°30'

The prime determinant of marriage, Venus, is very weak as it is closely afflicted by Mercury, badly placed and is in extreme old age. Mercury ruling the sixth house is badly placed and debilitated and makes her vulnerable to nervous setbacks and loss of confidence. Jupiter is a strong planet in this chart but it could not help as it is not influencing the houses signifying marriage. The husband died in the sub-period of the utterly weak Venus in the main period of the functional malefic planet, Rahu, which is placed in the malefic sixth house, at the age of 29 years.

Chart 56

Female born 22nd September 1959, 1520 Hrs. 77E13 28N39, India.

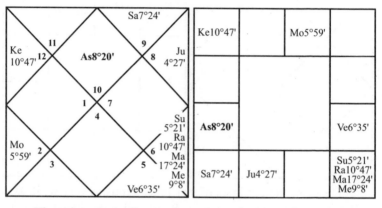

The prime determinant of marriage, the Moon becomes weak as its mooltrikona sign house is closely afflicted by two functional malefic planets. The weak lord of the seventh house also suffers from the close afflicting aspect of Jupiter and Rahu. The general significator of marriage, Venus, is badly placed. The most malefic planet, the Sun, in this nativity closely afflicts the ninth house and the lord of the ninth house. The lord of the ninth house is combust and also closely afflicted by Rahu and Ketu. The lord of the second house, Saturn, ruling family life is badly placed in the house of losses. The lord of the fourth house is well placed but weak due to combustion, weakness of its dispositor and placement in an afflicted house. The afflictions in the chart prevailed over the good placement of the Moon, the prime determinant of marriage, as the operating planets bestow results of their impacts in the chart. Jupiter, the significator for husband, is well placed but its role as a functional malefic planet comes to fore. In this case, the husband died in the sub-period of Ketu in the main period of Rahu.

Chart 57

Female born 5th February 1964, 2350 Hrs. 77E13 28N39, India.

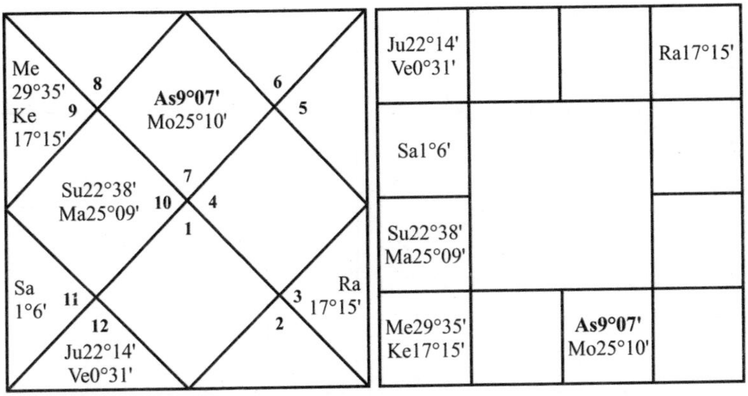
Me 29°35'
Ke 17°15'
8
9
As9°07'
Mo25°10'
6
5
7
Su22°38'
Ma25°09'
10
4
1
Sa 1°6'
11
12
Ju22°14'
Ve0°31'
3
2
Ra 17°15'
Ju22°14'
Ve0°31'
Ra17°15'
Sa1°6'
Su22°38'
Ma25°09'
Me29°35'
Ke17°15'
As9°07'
Mo25°10'

The lord of the seventh house, Mars, is in the state of combustion and hence weak. The general significator of marriage, Venus, is badly placed and is in the state of utter infancy. As Sagittarius rises in navamsa, Jupiter, besides being the significator of husband, also becomes a additional prime determinant of marriage and married life. Jupiter is weak as it is badly placed and debilitated in navamsa. The most malefic planet ruling the twelfth house, signifying the longevity of the married life, in this case, is weak due to extreme old age.

The weakness of all the significators of marriage denies long-lived married life. During the sub-period of the weak Mercury in its own main period, the native lost her husband.

Chart 58

Female born 1st November 1951, 1235 Hrs. 80E36 16N13, India.

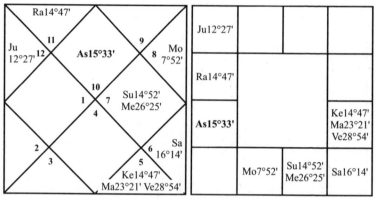

The debilitated lord of the seventh house is well placed and unafflicted. The lord of the fourth house is badly placed and becomes weak. The lord of the second house is well placed but weak due to affliction by the functional malefic planet, Jupiter, and weakness of its dispositor. The lord of the twelfth house, Jupiter, is well placed and well aspected. Venus is badly placed in the eighth house in the state of old age. The lord of the eighth house, the most malefic planet, closely aspects and afflicts the most effective point of the fourth house. The functional malefic, Jupiter, closely afflicts the most effective point of the seventh house. Rahu and Ketu closely afflict the various houses representing the marital affairs. Rahu aspects and causes and exact affliction to the Sun.

The weakness and afflictions show curtailed longevity of married life. The native lost her husband in the sub-period of Rahu in the main period of Venus. At the time of death of the husband, the transit Jupiter was afflicting the fourth lord, Mars, placed in the eighth house.

Chart 59

Female born 1st November 1959, 0900 Hrs. 77E02 29N42, India.

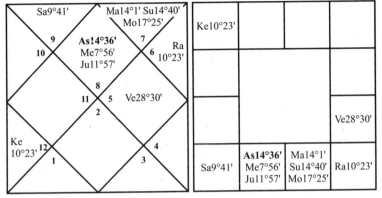

Mars, Venus, Rahu and Ketu are the functional malefic planets for those born in the Scorpio ascendant. The seventh house suffers from an exact aspect from badly placed functional malefic planet, Mars. The seventh house is also closely afflicted by Rahu. Jupiter, being the prime determinant and significator of marriage, is strong and closely influences the seventh house. The lord of the fourth house is also strong. Besides being in old age and weak, the other general significator of marriage, Venus, is very weak as its mooltrikona sign house is exactly afflicted by Mars. The dispositor of Venus, the Sun, is very weak as it is debilitated, placed in the afflicted twelfth house and in total conjunction with the functional malefic planet, Mars. Besides being 100% combust and badly placed Mars is very weak as it is placed in an afflicted house. Mars exactly afflicts the most effective point of the seventh house besides closely afflicting the weak Sun and weak Moon.

The weaknesses and afflictions showed curtailed longevity of married life. The native lost her husband during the sub-period of Mars in the main period of Saturn. **Between the main period lord and the sub-period lord, the sub-period lord plays the major role.**

We hope the above case studies will help the readers in comprehending the analytical techniques. When this analysis is done before marriage the application of preventive remedies will surely be of help. That is the best help of the divine science to the mankind.

Chapter 9

Identifying Stability in Marriage

Which is the field where astrological advice is not required? Be it the matter of health, longevity, education, profession, business, choosing a friend, choosing a partner in business or in life (spouse) for one's own self or for one's nears and dears. Today due to the multidimensional skills/professions and the world becoming a global village, it is not possible to finalize marital alliance in the known circles or in one's own city, dynasty or even caste.

In marital affairs the matters of concern are mental and physical compatibility, health of the couple, their mutual relationship, their post marital financial prosperity, birth of children, their staying together, etc. No branch of knowledge other than the birth chart astrology helps us in exploring the mysteries of life. The active years of one's life are the most important years of one's life for one's notable contribution to the society. Unsuccessful married life ruins the life and mental peace of the couple, brings them to the level of insanity and causes untold miseries to the couple, their friends and relatives. **To charter one's way happily into the deep sea of uncertainties in married life, one should utilize the benefit of the only real science of the world and that is the divine science of astrology.**

Astrological analysis of an individual's life, as indicated earlier, is taken up through the noted position of the planets for the birth time of the individual concerned with reference to the place and date of birth. The linkages amongst the planets are created through the conjunctions, aspects and placements of the planets with reference to the rising sign and the degree of the ascendant in a natal chart (the horoscope). The relationship of the planets amongst themselves and their nature towards the individual also depend on the planets owning particular houses with reference to the ascending sign. The result of the planets is seen with reference to the operating planetary period at the time of the birth and the current planetary movement of the planets with reference to the natal planets.

The health of the person is seen from the first and sixth houses and the significator of health. The bondage between the family lives is seen through the second and eighth houses and the planet, Venus. The status and family prosperity is seen through the second house, the Sun and Jupiter. The mental and post marital harmony is seen through the fourth house and the Moon. The details of the spouse are seen through the seventh house and the planet Venus in the case of males and Jupiter in the case of females. The continuance of marital tie, as explained above, is seen from the second and the eighth houses. The staying together of the couple is seen through the twelfth house. The progeny matters are seen from the fifth house. **For judging the results of a house, we consider the influences on the concerned house, the position of its lord and the planet(s) functioning as 'significators' for it.**

To meet the complex requirements of present life, we have to examine the planetary position in each case on all the aforementioned parameters in isolation, as well as, collectively.

Under the Systems' Approach for astral analysis the consideration of effectiveness of the conjunctions and aspects with reference to the planets and the most effective points of various houses is a very vital aspect/factor and these have been explained earlier in the book.

Based on the above guidelines, besides the significator and the influences on the houses mentioned above, for various ascendants the planets owning the houses containing the mooltrikona signs are considered for identifying stability in marital relationship. The details of the planets to be considered are mentioned hereunder:

Aries	Mars, the Moon, the Sun and Venus.
Taurus	The Sun, Mercury, Jupiter and Mars.
Gemini	The Moon, Mercury Venus and Jupiter.
Cancer	The Moon, The Sun, Venus and Saturn.
Leo	The Sun, Mercury, Jupiter, Saturn and the Moon.
Virgo	Mercury, Venus, Jupiter, Mars and the Sun.
Libra	Venus, Saturn, Mars and Mercury.
Scorpio	Jupiter, Saturn and Venus.
Sagittarius	Jupiter, Mars and the Moon.
Capricorn	Saturn, Mars, the Moon, the Sun and Jupiter.
Aquarius	Saturn, the Sun and Mercury.
Pisces	Mars, the Moon, Mercury, Venus and Saturn.

When the houses, first, second, fourth, fifth, seventh, eighth and twelfth besides the planets mentioned above for a particular ascendant are afflicted, the married life of the person during the sub-periods of weak/badly placed/afflicted and afflicting planets suffers.

We proceed with the analysis of a horoscope by identifying the strength of planets, their placements, conjunctions/aspects, the operating sub-periods as well as the ensuing planetary periods. The weak and/or afflicted functional benefic planets are strengthened to ward off the evil influences of planetary influences so that the various problems of married life are reduced to the minimum and the purpose of marriage is achieved.

Now with the help of the case studies we shall discuss the charts of persons, who suffered on account of marital problems due to non utilization of the services of the divine science of astrology.

Chart 60

Male born 25th November 1963, 1115 hrs., 88E21 22N35, India.

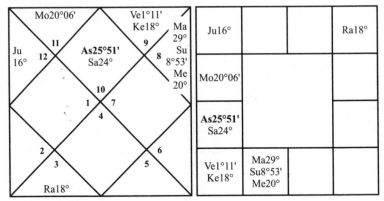

For Capricorn ascendant we have to consider Saturn, Mars, Moon, Sun and Jupiter besides the significator for spouse and the houses dealing with marital happiness. The planets Moon, Mercury, Mars and Venus are weak. The Moon is closely afflicted by the aspect of Rahu from the house of disputes. The marriage was solemnized in February, 1995, and was followed by immediate divorce proceedings. The notable thing is that the afflicting planet was placed in the house of disputes and its sub-period was running at the time of the marriage.

Chart 61

Female born 12th March 1965, 2330 hrs., 67E00 24N53, Pakistan.

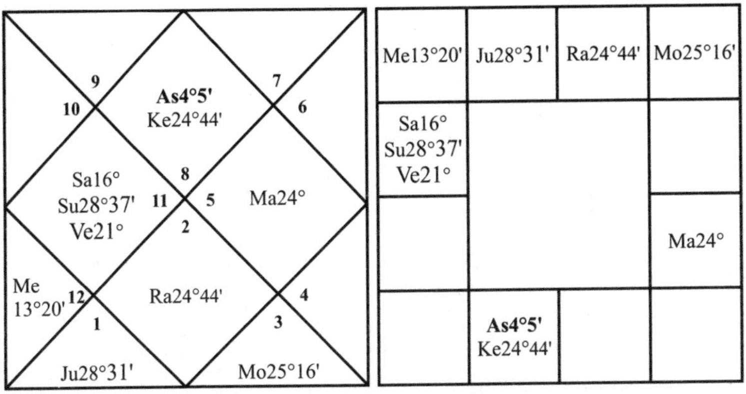
9
7
10
As4°5'
Ke24°44'
6
Sa16°
Su28°37'
Ve21°
8
11
5
Ma24°
2
Me
13°20'
12
Ra24°44'
4
1
3
Ju28°31'
Mo25°16'
Me13°20'
Ju28°31'
Ra24°44'
Mo25°16'
Sa16°
Su28°37'
Ve21°
Ma24°
As4°5'
Ke24°44'

For Scorpio ascendant the planets Jupiter, Saturn and Venus are required to be considered besides the significators for spouse and the houses dealing with marital happiness. The planet Venus is closely afflicted by the functional malefic lord of the house of disputes, Mars. The lord of the second house Jupiter, ruling family, is placed in the house of disputes. The marriage was solemnized in the sub-period of a weak planet, Mercury, and the divorce was finalized in the sub-period of Venus.

Chart 62

Female born 14th April 1961, 0840 hrs. 74E45, 24N14, India.

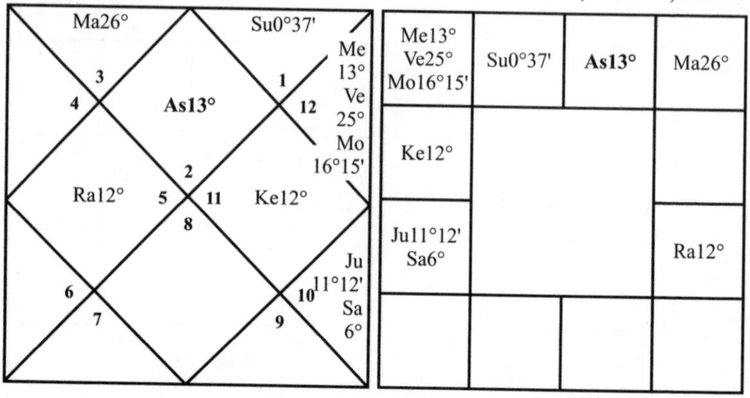
Ma26°
Su0°37'
Me 13° Ve 25° Mo 16°15'
3
4
1
12
As13°
2
Ra12°
5
11
Ke12°
8
Ju 11°12' Sa 6°
6
10
7
9
Me13° Ve25° Mo16°15'
Su0°37'
As13°
Ma26°
Ke12°
Ju11°12' Sa6°
Ra12°

For Taurus ascendant we have to consider the planets Sun, Mercury, Jupiter and Mars besides the significator of spouse and the houses ruling the marital happiness. The lord of the fourth house, the Sun, is weak as it is badly placed in utter infancy and the most effective point of the fourth house is closely afflicted by Rahu and Ketu. The significator for husband, Jupiter, is debilitated. The lady was being harassed by her mother-in-law and the husband could not protect the wife. The sub-period of the weak significator of husband, Jupiter, was in operation.

Chart 63

Female born 14th September 1970, 1515 hrs. 77E13 28N39, India.

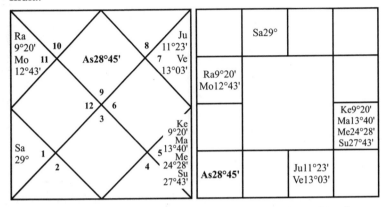

For Sagittarius ascendant we have to consider the planets Jupiter, Mars and the Moon besides the significator of spouse and the houses ruling the marital happiness. The Moon, Jupiter and Mars are closely afflicted. The male child of the native is suffering from multiple health problems. The lady herself suffered on account of problems in business. Her husband also suffered from problems. Jupiter is significator of the husband which is under the close aspect of Rahu. The problems started in the sub-period of Mars and Rahu in the main period of Jupiter.

Chart 64

Female born 8th October 1971, 0314 hrs. 77E42 29N00, India.

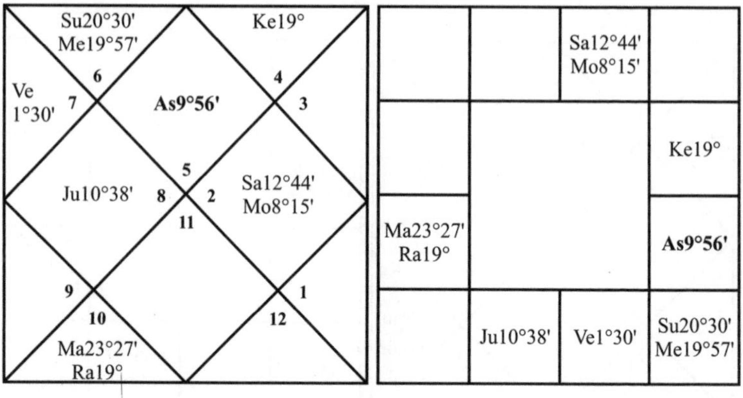
Su20°30'
Me19°57'
Ke19°
Ve
1°30'
6
7
4
3
As9°56'
5
Ju10°38'
8
2
Sa12°44'
Mo8°15'
11
9
1
10
12
Ma23°27'
Ra19°
Sa12°44'
Mo8°15'
Ke19°
Ma23°27'
Ra19°
As9°56'
Ju10°38'
Ve1°30'
Su20°30'
Me19°57'

For Leo ascendant we have to consider the planets Sun, Mercury, Jupiter, Saturn and the Moon besides the significator of spouse and the houses ruling the marital happiness. The planets, the Sun and Mercury, are closely afflicted due to the close aspect of the malefic Rahu from the sixth house. Jupiter, the significator for husband, and Saturn are placed in afflicted houses and are under the close affliction of the most malefic planet, the Moon. The problems in marriage started in the sub-period of Rahu in its own main period.

Chart 65

Female born 10th February 1966, 1721 hrs., 77E13 28N39, India.

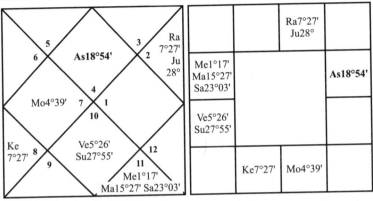

For Cancer ascendant we have to consider the planets Moon, Sun, Venus and Saturn besides the significator of spouse and the houses ruling the marital happiness. The lord of the second house, the Sun, is under the exact affliction of the lord of the sixth house, the functional malefic planet, Jupiter. The most effective point of the second house is closely afflicted by the most malefic planet, Saturn. The inharmonious relationship persists and the husband takes interest outside the marital bond. The problem was at tolerable level when the sub-period of the unafflicted and well placed Moon was running. The astral remedies were suggested so that these can take care of the pressure in the sub-periods of afflicting planets. As the lord of the house of marital tie, Saturn, is placed in its own mooltrikona sign the marital tie was expected to continue with the help of remedial measures. The native did not perform the astral remedies as suggested and the marriage ended in a divorce.

Chart 66

Male born 21st March 1959, 0625 hrs. 77E13 28N39, India.

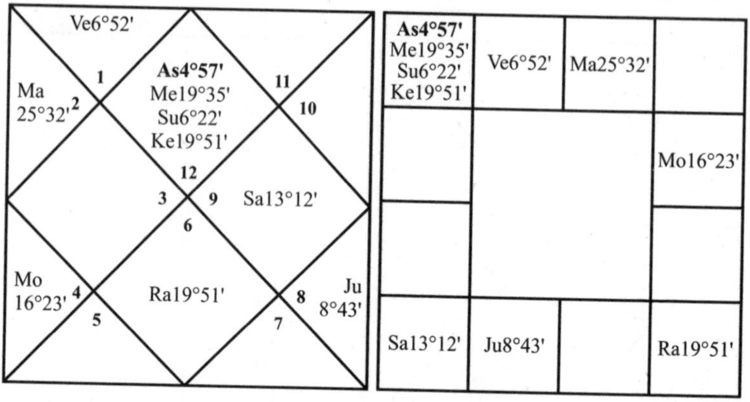
Ve6°52'
1
Ma 25°32' 2
As4°57'
Me19°35'
Su6°22'
Ke19°51'
11
10
12
3
9
Sa13°12'
6
Mo 16°23' 4
5
Ra19°51'
8
7
Ju 8°43'
As4°57'
Me19°35'
Su6°22'
Ke19°51'
Ve6°52'
Ma25°32'
Mo16°23'
Sa13°12'
Ju8°43'
Ra19°51'

For Pisces ascendant we have to consider the planets Mars, Moon, Mercury, Venus and Saturn besides the significator of spouse and the houses ruling the marital happiness. The functional malefic Sun afflicts the most effective points of the ascendant and the seventh house. This one influence is indicative of inharmonious relationship. The lord of the seventh house, Mercury, is weak due to debilitation and is severely afflicted due to the exact conjunction of Ketu. This affliction of Ketu to Mercury in isolation is indicative of termination of the marital relationship. The functional malefic Venus afflicts the most effective point of the second house. The affliction of the most malefic planet to the most effective point of the second house is indicative of divorce. There were numerous problems in marriage pertaining to separation and inharmonious relationship besides the health problems to the native during the sub-period of the afflicting planets, Venus, the Sun and Rahu in the main period of Venus. The sub-period of strong Jupiter saw some improvements and the couple was united. Astral remedies were also sought for further improvements. In such cases, strengthening measures are suggested for the weak and/or afflicted planets and the charities are suggested for propitiating the afflicting planets.

Conclusion

Marital problems could have been averted in the cases mentioned above based on the simple astral analytic techniques brought out in this chapter of the book. The consultation seekers are advised on the suitability of the intended matches and astral remedies are suggested to take care of the afflictions and planetary weaknesses for a successful marriage.

Chapter 10

Identifying Criminal Tendencies

The close influence of Rahu and the lords of the sixth and twelfth houses, if containing mooltrikona signs, in the birth chart give criminal tendencies. The influence of the lord of the sixth house on other planets / houses or the placement of the lord of ascendant or second or third or tenth house in the sixth house gives aggressive tendency to the person. If these aggressive tendency giving planets are also under the close influence of Rahu or Rahu like planets one becomes vulnerable to commit criminal act. The closely afflicted planets in sixth houses also make the person vulnerable to state action. The close influence of Rahu, specially from the malefic houses, is capable of giving all types of anti-social, anti-law and immoral temptations. These temptations are executed by strong influence of Mars or Rahu, especially when Mars is a functional malefic planet, on the ascendant, third house or the tenth house. When the lord of the sixth house or third house or the Sun or Mars are placed in the twelfth house and are under close affliction of Rahu or Rahu like planet, one becomes vulnerable to action by state or imprisonment. **Identification of criminal tendencies is a very useful technique while considering a match for marital alliance, admitting a partner in a partnership and employing somebody for one's business venture.**

The influence of a planet is exercised by that planet through placement, conjunction and aspect. The lord of the twelfth house gives vices and intensifies the need for gratification of sensual pleasures for which a person may like to earn a lot of money through gambling, cheating and/or any other means disapproved by the society. The lord of the second house rules status and reputation. The lord of the sixth house gives aggressive inclination for deceptive dealings or raising disputes for personal gains.

Then the malefic influence has to be seen on the houses and planets and has to be synchronized with the operating planetary periods. The houses involved are first, second, third, fourth, tenth, twelfth and the sixth while the planets involved are the Sun, the Moon, Venus and Jupiter. Strong Jupiter and the Sun may be able to fight temptations. Transit influence on the weak planets becoming significators for the criminal activities trigger the event. Some amount of such tendencies may be found in the majority of human beings, but one is booked/charged and has to suffer from imprisonment due to the close relationship of the lord of the twelfth house and if such afflictions are occurring in the Scorpio and Pisces signs. The affliction to the Sun indicates trouble through the state while affliction to the Moon indicates a troubled mind.

Let us see it through some illustrations:

Chart 67

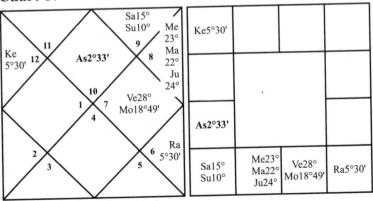

The lord of the twelfth house, Jupiter, closely influences the lords of the fourth and ninth houses. The Sun is placed in the twelfth house. Rahu closely afflicts the ascendant. The native was charged for criminal conspiracy for theft and was arrested in the sub-period of Rahu in the main period of Saturn.

Chart 68

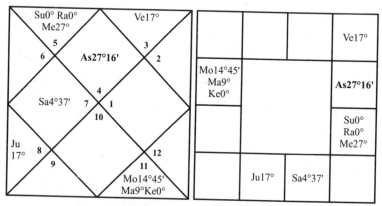

The most effective point of the ascendant and the Sun are closely afflicted by Rahu. Ketu closely afflicts Saturn. The lord of the ascendant and Mars are placed in the eighth house which is a Rahu-like house. The lord of the fourth house is placed in the twelfth house. Though not near the most effective point of the fourth house yet Saturn being lord of the eighth house is placed in the fourth house. Mercury ruling the third house exerts its exact influence on the second house and raises the intensity of desire to implement one's plans.

During the sub-period of Rahu in the main period of Mercury, the person murdered his wife for which he was convicted and sentenced to life imprisonment.

Chart 69

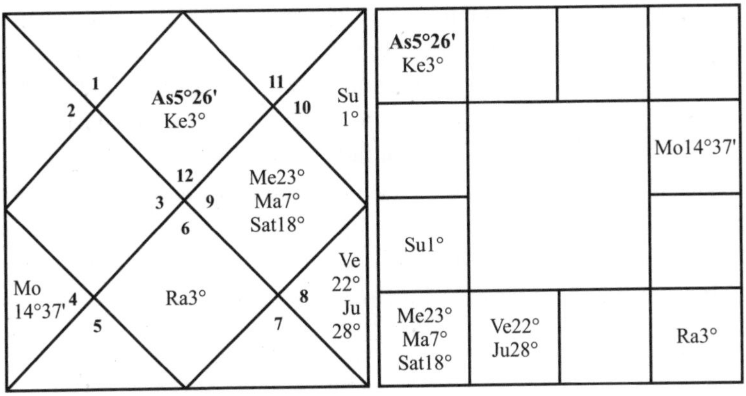

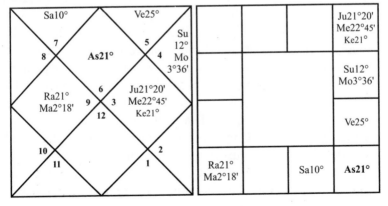

This person murdered three persons in a fit of anger and was arrested. Property disputes triggered this violence.

Rahu closely afflicts the lord of the sixth house and the most effective point of the ascendant and the third house. Rahu-Ketu axis is on the most effective point of the houses and afflicts the houses occupied and aspected. Besides the Sun, Jupiter is quite weak in the nativity. At the time of the murder, transiting Ketu was afflicting the natal ascendant, Sun and Ketu by way of an aspect.

Chart 70

This chart belongs to an alleged manipulator. Venus, Jupiter and Mercury are under the close influence of Rahu. Rahu-Ketu axis is on the most effective point of the houses of their location and afflicts the houses occupied and aspected. The lord of the eighth house is closely afflicting the Moon in this nativity. The lord of the second house is badly placed in the twelfth house and afflicted by Rahu. The lord of the sixth house is placed in the second house and is closely afflicting the lord of the twelfth house. His so-called manipulations came to light in the sub-period of the Sun and the Moon in the main period of Ketu.

Chart 71

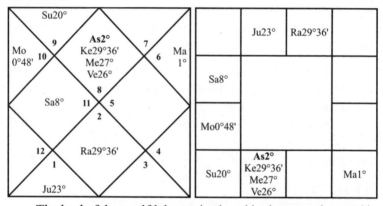

The lord of the twelfth house is placed in the ascendant and is closely afflicted by Rahu. Both Rahu and the lord of the twelfth house are closely afflicting Mercury placed in the ascendant. The functional malefic Mars closely afflicts the most effective point of the second house ruling status and the most effective point of the fifth house ruling inclinations. The lord of the second house has gone to the house of disputes. During the sub-periods of Rahu and Jupiter, the native was involved in numerous controversies and was defamed. Later during the sub-period of Saturn he was criminally charged for cheating and serious legal complications continued through the sub-period of Mercury, Ketu and Venus in the main period of Rahu.

Chart 72

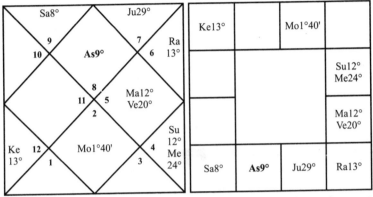

The native was tried for indulging in criminal activities and was in serious trouble in the sub-period of Venus in the main period of Rahu. He could get relief only in the sub-period of the Moon in spite of contacts at higher levels. The functional malefic Mars closely afflicts the ascendant, tenth, fourth and fifth houses. The lord of the sixth house is closely conjunct with the most effective point of the tenth house. Rahu-Ketu axis is on the most effective point of the houses and afflicts the houses occupied and aspected besides afflicting the Sun. The lord of the second house has gone to the twelfth house. His marital life was disturbed and he was addicted to all types of vices in the main period of Mars. During the sub-period of Rahu in its own main period, the native's initiative brought him to the company of people of questionable character and landed him in trouble. The placement of lord of fourth on the most effective point of the second house conferred good amount of wealth on the native through his parental resources and help in professional matters.

Chapter 11

Relevance of Vastu to Astrology

Vastu has a great bearing on the health, wealth and spiritual growth of the person. The knowledge of Vastu Shastra is the ancient wisdom on architecture. Vastu knowledge and its application blends nature with man-made creations for peaceful living. Its application is in all fields - residential, commercial, learning institutions, temples, meditation centers and industrial units.

Vastu read in conjunction with astrology plays a significant role in the life of a person both in his residential and business operations. The directions, main entrance, flow of air, light, colors on the walls, fabric used for curtains - its color and design, layout of various facilities and the placement of stairs are the main constituents of Vastu. The color on the walls and the lighting systems change not only the decor of the house and business premises but influence the future of living/business. These have to be in consonance / harmoniousness with the suitability of the colors to the individual, owner and users.

Vastu is a preventive as well as a curative therapy for solving the problems in physical and spiritual areas. Wider applications of this therapy are in the field of success of professional ventures. This is practiced through the use of proper outlay of a building to derive geo-magnetic forces for properly energizing the total impact of that building with the help of light, air, space and aura conducive to the main function of the environment.

We all know that a dwelling unit, whether it is a small house or a royal mansion, is built for safety, security and esteem of the family living in it. It is also occupied for physical health, mental health, prosperity and spiritual development of the persons living in it. The happiness of the individuals depends upon the planetary periods of the individuals and the sound vibrations of the house.

A common question posed to a Vastu Shastri is whether a house constructed as per the Vastu guidelines would be as auspicious for the son and the grandson as it has been for the person who built that house. The answer invariably is that with some changes necessitated by the birth chart of the individuals (son or grandson and other family members) it is auspicious. Then the next question arises as to whether Vastu is important or is it only a fashion. Vastu is very important. Living in a Vastu compliant house blesses the person with happiness, peace, prosperity and spiritual development. Wrong placement of toilets can bring the incidence of life threatening health concerns and stomach disorders ultimately telling upon the longevity of the head of the family. Wrong placement of bedrooms can bring the incidence of mental stress, depression and sleep disorders. Wrong openings can bring the incidence of disputes and denial of birth of a male child.

The basic components of a dwelling unit are the building, the passage, the lighting arrangement and its location, besides its maintenance and cleanliness. The building laws impose many restrictions. The availability of land as per one's desire and requirement is also not possible in the present times. The Vastu factor stands modified due to the painting and lighting inside the house in spite of the basic structure and airy passage remaining the same. The various planets during their planetary periods create different types of impact on the outlook of persons in matters of brightness and colors. These indeed change the overall effect of the dwelling unit.

It is important to have maximum benefit of the dwelling unit, which is derived through natural inflow of the sunlight and air. The provision for these basic necessities can be made if a house is facing east and its doors and windows open in the southeast, southwest and western directions. This will help in the influence of the sunlight on the house throughout the day. Persons living in such a house will be optimistic and energetic. Besides the basic structure, the light and bright color on the walls and door panels help in mental happiness, which is possible during the periods of strong and well placed planets like Jupiter, Venus and Mercury. It will give a hygienic, clean and decorative outlook while the influence of Rahu may make the man dubious and deceptive in character. He may use dark colors on the walls, corners or candle lights. Saturn in its weak state makes the man feel insecure and he lacks confidence. As the person's stress is on savings in life, he/she uses dark shades on the walls and door panels to save money on maintenance and this creates a stuffy atmosphere.

The result of the maintenance and the shades on the walls and door frames/panels may be different. While the light and bright shades bring in prosperity and enlarge the social circle, dark and stuffy shades isolate the person from society and thrust upon him/her unstable and insecure attitudes in life.

For example, once a gentleman contacted us about the inordinate delay in finalization of the marriage of his daughter. The visit to their house showed that though the house was east-facing, its openings were on the north-east, north-west and west side and he was using a pretty dark blue shade on the walls of his drawing room and navy-blue paint on his door panels. Our suggestion for change of shades on the walls and the door panels helped in early settlement of the marriage of his daughter.

In another case, a medico who had set up an ultrasound diagnostic center was not getting clients, resulting in a loss by way of expenses on the maintenance of fixed assets. During the course of a visit to the clinic, it was found that the desired space was not provided for in the waiting lounge and instead of the mercury tube-lights, the lighting was done with incandescent bulbs. The lighting arrangement with bulbs makes the atmosphere a little gloomy and one cannot tolerate this atmosphere while waiting. Slight modifications of space in the waiting lounge and provision of tube lights resulted in a growing clientele.

The minimum vastu to be kept in view is:

1. That the house is east facing. Next best is west facing but there should be openings in the east direction, as well. The houses facing south and north should better be avoided. The place of meditation is in the north east direction;

2. Bedrooms in south and south west;

3. Children's study in north;

4. Kitchen in south east;

5. Stairs in south-west;

6. Heavy structures in the house in south-west;

7. One should sleep with one's head in east, or south or south west directions;

8. The central place of the residential unit should be empty;

9. There should be openings in east and west and it would be better if the opening is also in south direction;

10. The opening only in south direction creates conflicts and diseases while the openings only in north direction stops family prosperity and sometimes even continuity. Opening only in the west direction brings poverty.

11. The place should be properly lit and pastel colors of functional benefic planets should be used on the walls;

12. The furnishings should be mostly plain or with very little flowery designs. In any case the patterns and designs on the fabric should not be too imposing.

Let me share with you a case study showing how a Vastu Consultant not knowing Astrology can harm the person.

A gentleman consulted a Vastu Consultant at the time of construction of his house and at the time of shifting to the house after construction. This Vastu Consultant was not an astrologer. The Vastu Consultant asked the person to shift to the new house on 20th November, 2007. On 20th November, 2007, the sister of the person died and he could not shift. He shifted to the new house as per advice of the Vastu Consultant on 24th November, 2007. Soon after shifting the native started facing problems including health problems to self, wife and daughter. The native started suffering from spine problem. The native lost his mother in May, 2008, and also lost his mother in law in October, 2008. His daughter also developed the spine problem. His wife developed depression, suffered from edema, diabetes, and became over-weight.

It was at this stage when the native thought of consulting a person who knows astrology and Vastu, both. He searched the internet and found about us. The chart of the native is shown below.

Chart 73

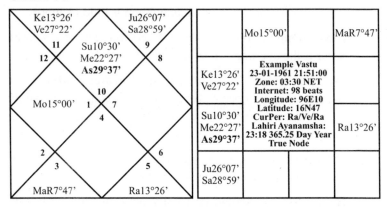

The sign Capricorn rises in the chart of the native. The planets Rahu, Ketu, Jupiter and the Sun are functional malefic planets for the native. The native started the sub period of Saturn from 24th August, 2006, in the main period of Rahu. Saturn is placed in the twelfth house ruling losses and Saturn is under the close affliction of Jupiter ruling the house of losses and expenses. Since the Vastu Consultant did not know astrology he could not guide the person on the astrology aspect of the affliction of Jupiter to Saturn in his birth chart. He could not suggest and provide the astrology remedies to reduce the impact of planetary afflictions in the birth chart. At the time of seeking the consultation from an Astrologer, the transit and natal Jupiter were afflicting closely the sub period lord Saturn, placed in the eighth house. Had his Vastu Consultant been knowledgeable on Systems' Approach Astrology, he could have benefited the native.

It is important that one always consults a Vastu Expert who knows astrology, as well.

Chapter 12

Relocation Through Astrology

There is a wide application of the divine science of astrology in each and every aspect of life. It helps in maintenance of good health, acquisition of good academic and professional qualifications, handling emotional stability, planning and management of business enterprises, timing of investments for greater returns, implementation of advertisement campaigns, relocation, change of residence, etc.

Let us see the astrological factors for urge and movement of people with the intention of changing homes, cities, states, continents, etc. These urges are necessitated by good quality of life, acquisition of good professional and academic qualifications, participating in researches, scientific and technical advancements, participating in managing the governmental and international affairs, joining special industries like entertainment, hotel, finances and international or regional commercial centers. Sometimes people just want a change for their fortunes or a greater mental peace. Some people follow relocation astrology through living near the planetary lines running the geographical areas. The need for decision to move or relocate may arise on account of the any of the fore mentioned reasons. The need may also arise out of compulsions of profession, business, following one's interests, acquisition of competencies, enjoying a luxurious life, participating in adventurous and high risk and high reward games, etc.

The decision of relocation is very important and needs a proper and systematic analysis of the planetary influences in one's natal chart to ensure success.

The elements involved are opportunities and compulsions. Both the opportunities and compulsions are indicated through placement of planets and their strengths in the natal chart.

The planets ruling self, native place, enterprises and status placed in the houses ruling foreign residences and journeys offer opportunities and urges for relocation to follow acquisition of competencies and capabilities, tastes, learning, growing and harnessing talent.

While the strong and well placed planets in the chart in their own periods induce tastes, pursuits and movements as per their own characteristics or direction the weak planets precipitate compulsive moves based on their placement in the natal chart.

The inter-relationship of first, second, third, fourth, fifth, seventh and tenth houses with seventh, ninth, twelfth and eighth houses entail relocation.

The Sun rules the east direction. The Sun rules the seat of governmental power and spiritual knowledge.

The Moon rules the northwest direction. The Moon rules blessings through the seat of power and comforts.

Mars rules the south direction. Mars rules armed forces, project erection and law enforcing agencies.

Mercury rules the north direction. Mercury rules the communications, research and commercial centers.

Jupiter rules the north-east direction. Jupiter rules legal and financial hubs of administration besides the spiritual advancement centers.

Venus rules the south-east direction. Venus rules places which are famous for art, talent, creativity, finances, luxury, pleasure centers and films.

Saturn rules the west direction. Saturn rules mines, big projects, distant places and labor intensive projects.

Rahu rules the South-West direction. Rahu rules places known for fast and risky trading, gambling, manipulations, etc.

Ketu rules the upward direction and places famous for mystical knowledge and spirituality.

The combined influence of strong Sun, Venus and Jupiter may offer opportunities in govening, managing and managing international affairs. The combined influence of strong Mercury, Mars and Saturn may bring opportunities and achievements in the field of scientific and technical innovations.

Important

An astrological advice in matters of relocation astrology is the function of planetary placements, strengths, forthcoming planetary periods and transit influences. A proper analysis with the astrological remedial advice can certainly be a much better relocation decision. Needless to add that those who are impelled by gods are blessed and they make use of the divine science of astrology for a better life, new energy, spiritual growth and self-realization.

Chapter 13

Pearls of Wisdom for Spiritual Growth

God lives in the hearts of those who have no lust, anger, arrogance and pride and those, who are without greed, excitement, aversion or attraction and are free from fraud, hypocrisy and deceit.

God lives in the hearts of those who always think God as their master, companion, father, mother, preceptor and everything.

For peace and enjoying the bliss, we can follow the Pearls of Wisdom.

1. Patience is very important in life and at all times. It is the greatest virtue.

2. If there is a mistake or misunderstanding one should not hesitate to accept.

3. There is always some scope of learning. Never say 'No'; to learning.

4. Wise people ignore the acts of foolish persons.

5. Anger, greed, encroaching tendencies, pride and lust make a person blind.

6. For literary/intellectual understanding/creativity one requires:

Intelligence

Imagination

Exploratory mind

Concentration

Patience

Confidence

Objectivity

Some more pearls from Ramayana, the epic:

1. While describing the character of saints (holy persons) and those who are unholy, Sant Tulsidas, the author of Ramayana, says that the holy persons give happiness to others while the unholy persons live for making others unhappy. So, those learning and practicing astrology should follow the conduct of holy persons.

2. Ramayana says that without going into the merits of advice or sayings, one should follow the advice of one's parents; guru (teacher) and god, as this always blesses the person with happiness and peace.

3. Those who do not respect or heed to their parents and God and those who seek service from holy persons are just demons. Such persons always cause sufferings to others and perish after experiencing sufferings in life.

4. While patience and self-control are necessary for being successful and peaceful in life, generosity remains a virtue, above all.

In Ramayana, lord Rama says, "Only those who are simple find me. I do not like those who are involved in manipulations and cheating."